T0208731

Eternal Love
MEANS God Is for Us

Dr. George P. Kimber

WESTBOW
P R E S S®
A DIVISION OF THOMAS NELSON
& ZONDERVAN

Scriptures taken from the Holy Bible, New International Version®, NIV®.
Copyright © 1973, 1978, 1984, 2011 by Biblica, Inc.™ Used by permission
of Zondervan. All rights reserved worldwide. www.zondervan.com The
"NIV" and "New International Version" are trademarks registered
in the United States Patent and Trademark Office by Biblica, Inc.

WestBow Press books may be ordered through booksellers or by contacting:

WestBow Press
A Division of Thomas Nelson & Zondervan
1663 Liberty Drive
Bloomington, IN 47403
www.westbowpress.com
1 (866) 928-1240

Because of the dynamic nature of the Internet, any web addresses or
links contained in this book may have changed since publication and
may no longer be valid. The views expressed in this work are solely those
of the author and do not necessarily reflect the views of the publisher,
and the publisher hereby disclaims any responsibility for them.

Any people depicted in stock imagery provided by Getty Images are
models, and such images are being used for illustrative purposes only.
Certain stock imagery © Getty Images.

ISBN: 978-1-9736-5421-6 (sc)
ISBN: 978-1-9736-5423-0 (hc)
ISBN: 978-1-9736-5422-3 (e)

Library of Congress Control Number: 2019901927

Print information available on the last page.

WestBow Press rev. date: 02/19/2019

Dedication

To my dear friend and colleague in the ministry for many years, Dr. Ray Hock. Your support of me over the years and our times together have always been a joy and profit to my life. Your loyalty to and ministry for Christ has been an example and inspiration to me.

Contents

Foreword...ix

Preface xi

Acknowledgments xv

Introduction.. xvii

Part 1: Evidence That God Is for Us in the Old Testament

Chapter 1:   The Creation and Fall, the Flood,
             and the Tower of Babel 1

Chapter 2:   The Patriarchs: Abraham, Isaac, Jacob, and Joseph 7

Chapter 3:   Moses: God's Instrument to Reveal God Is for Us 15

Chapter 4:   God's Providence Revealed in Judges and Ruth 21

Chapter 5:   God's Providence through the Age of the Prophets 27

Chapter 6:   God's Love for Us Extended to the Monarchy Period . 30

Chapter 7:   The Tragic Division of the Kingdom to Captivity 38

Chapter 8:   A Brief Focus on Two Major Prophets:
             Isaiah and Malachi 44

Part 2: Evidence That God Is for Us in the New Testament

Chapter 9:   The New Testament Revelation That God Is for
             Us Was the Jesus Advent............................. 49

Chapter 10: The Ministry of Jesus Christ.......................53

Chapter 11: The Death and Resurrection of Jesus Christ...............57

Chapter 12: The Holy Spirit at Pentecost and the Birth of
             the Church: The Apostolic Age (AD 30–100)............ 60

Part 3: Evidence That God Is for Us in the Church Age

Chapter 13: God Holds the Future................................. 69

Chapter 14: The Development of the Church from AD 100–
             1517 and the Church under Roman Persecution
             (AD 100–313) 77

Part 4: Evidence That God Is for Us in the New World

Chapter 15: The Renaissance Period................................91
Chapter 16: The Need for a Development of Biblical Theology...... 96
Chapter 17: Bible and Theology Prompted the Development
of Preaching 99
Chapter 18: The Ministry of Evangelism and Revival...................105
Chapter 19: The Challenge of Modern World Missions.................107
Chapter 20: Issues of Our Present Day That Challenge Our
Faith in God 111
Chapter 21: Heaven: The Final Frontier of
Our Christian Journey.............................. 118
Chapter 22: The Incredible Reward of Our Future Perseverance ..123

Conclusion 127
Bibliography.. 131
About the Author... 133

Foreword

I'm convinced that the message of *Eternal Love Means God Is for Us* is one of the grandest and most important messages to be imparted to our culture today. This message has the power to release hope, healing, and health to your life. Embrace the truth embedded in the message of this book, and you will gain a perspective that sees every experience of your life as a gift from the Master's hand. Understanding God's sovereign care in your life will serve as an anchor for the soul that withstands the strongest of cultural currents and peer-generated riptides. The idea contained in the pages of this book is simple but has profound implications for how you decode life. How you interpret the day-to-day experiences of your life will impact the way you view God and how you interact with people around you. What if, in both the happiest and darkest moments of your life, you knew that the Sovereign of the universe was watching over you? I believe this message has the power to renew your mind and transform your heart.

The book that you hold in your hand is a life message. This is Dr. Kimber's life message coming to you through scripture and story. This is a teacher's walk through life with an open Bible demonstrating that the God of angel armies, revealed in scripture, is even now at work in your life arranging and shaping the details of your life for your good and God's glory. Here is a friend's encouragement to not fall prey to depression or despair, but rather to joyfully embrace all the promises of God. God, Himself, is at work in all your life situations. All the promises of God are "yes" in the person of Jesus.

It's been my privilege to spend hours in college classrooms, in coffee shops, and in the comfort of back porches at retreat centers listening to one of the best storytellers I know. George, in his typical self-deprecating manner, will tell you an incident from his past where he was absolutely sure all hope and goodness itself was lost, only to discover how God was out in front orchestrating events for his good. Run out of money and gas on an evangelistic road trip? Don't worry. It's only so God can display His provision and care in a more dramatic fashion. George's stories always end up encouraging you to laugh and marvel at God's goodness and provident timing. Time and time again I've been encouraged by George's stories to learn in new ways how to live life out of a response to God's grace, provision, and power rather than to operate out of loss and need.

The lessons in this book are for all believers who want to grow deeper and wiser in their trust in God's grace and sovereignty in their personal lives. I can think of no one who embodies this message and communicates this truth with greater integrity than Dr. Kimber. His personal experiences and application of scripture have a way of revealing God's heart and intention for you. I know this message will open up in new ways God's presence and power for living, for which you have been longing your entire life.

Rev. Dr. Ray D. Hock
Brother in Christ, missionary, pastor, and bishop

Preface

One of the most amazing revelations that I discovered in the Bible was that it wasn't just an ancient history book. I suddenly was confronted with the reality that God is actually present in this world from the beginning and to this present time and will be very present to the end of time. Genesis 1:1 says, "In the beginning God ..." What is involved in this beginning? What was its purpose? Was it just the creation of the world for His own pleasure? What was His purpose in creating Adam and the Eve? The scriptures reveal that God wanted to have people made in His image who would eventually be with Him forever in eternity. The Bible records His actions of moving through history to accomplish this in spite of all the ups and downs. Because of this determination, we can be assured that *God is with us and for us* while His will is being accomplished.

At this present time, our world is experiencing great upheavals of many kinds. Vicious attacks are being leveled at many of the world's citizens, creating a stream of refugees fleeing for their lives to other countries. This has created a great dilemma for those countries they desire to enter. There are ongoing, so-called suicide bombings taking place wherever crowds are gathered, resulting in senseless killings. Many of these are carried out under the guise of religious beliefs by those who are attempting to conquer the world in the name of their god. People of all nations are experiencing fear and uncertainty because of the lack of a defense system capable of protecting them. Our world needs new hope and assurance of a better future. It may appear that God is silent and not engaged in these times. *If God is for us, where is He?* I recently came upon an explanation of the theological term *providence* as "the Hand of God in the Glove of History" (Evans, 2009, 240), which would include both secular and Biblical history. Providence is the work of God whereby He directs and integrates events in the universe in order to fulfill His original design for that which He created. It refers to God's governance of all events so as to direct them toward His end of making all people understand that He is for them. This book will be moving through Biblical history to encourage you to take heart and not give up; know that God is for us! You will discover how God is constantly intervening for His will to prevail.

The writing of E. M. Bounds expresses this in a wonderful way: **God's Hand is in everything.... God can superintend and overrule earth's affairs for the good of man and His glory.... Nothing occurs by accident under the superintendence of an all-wise and perfectly just God. (2009, 214)**

A Personal Experience

I began my journey with Christ as a young man. The Lord blessed me with a wonderful Christian wife and a beautiful daughter. I dropped out of junior high school and at age seventeen joined the navy. Becoming a minister and teacher never entered my mind, but God had a different plan for my life. I attended a Bible college and, after graduating, spent several years as a traveling evangelist. This eventually led to my planting a church in the Midwest. With some experience under my belt, I was called to plant a second church on the West Coast in California. After a few years serving as supervisor, a man I respected and admired encouraged me to go on with my education with the intention of becoming a teacher. While this seemed to be a stretch for me, I believed God had His hand in it, and I wanted to be obedient to His will.

I attended a local Christian liberal arts college and obtained a bachelor's degree in biblical studies. While my Christian experience to that point had not been easy, I never doubted that God was for me. I enrolled in a nearby seminary and dove into my studies. It was challenging and at times difficult, as I was also pastoring and supporting a family at the same time. In spite of the circumstances, I persevered and completed three years of coursework. I had begun working on my thesis to finalize my seminary work when I was unexpectedly called to the dean's office. What I learned there turned my life upside down and rattled my faith. After having examined my academic record, the administration determined that I had not met the criteria set out for graduation, and I was dismissed from the seminary. I was devastated. Where was God in all this? Why had He allowed this to happen? *Where are you, God?* I wondered. After all, wasn't it His idea for me to pursue a teaching career? It seemed like God was no longer for me.

Thankfully, this was not the end of the story. God sent a caring and devoted professor to come alongside me and recommend me to another seminary. My graduate education took many twists and turns and culminated in my earning two master's degrees and a doctor of ministry degree. I then spent twenty-two years teaching biblical studies at a Christian liberal arts college. Today, at ninety-one years of age, I do much reflecting on all the times and ways *God truly has been for me!*

I wrote this book because, as I reflected on my life and ministry of over sixty years, I witnessed how much God was for me through all those years. Then, when I began to research the scriptures, I was amazed at how God intervened in every situation, revealing His love and care for people and that He was for them. Thus, we can be assured that God is for us today because of His eternal love. This does not mean that our journey of life is free of many hindrances. However, in our reflection of our journey, we will discover that God has a divine purpose for our life destiny.

Acknowledgments

I thank my dear daughter Nan Shrigley for being the primary editor of my book. She spent many hours bringing it together. Also, I thank my faithful loving wife, who helped me with profitable suggestions and continual encouragement along the way.

Introduction

**"If God is for us, who can be against us?" (Rom. 8:31)
God is for us; He has always been for us, and is for us now
and forever.**

When one considers world history, it appears that there is no
system or any line of connection running through it. Events and
leaders rise on the stage of history one after the other, displaying
greatness, and then fading away only to be forgotten. Some
periods in history experienced great progress followed by times
of deterioration culturally, economically, politically, morally,
and religiously. However, careful study of the Bible reveals that
Christianity has threaded itself through every period of history,
and God's hand was influencing all facets of society.

Observations and Predictions Present in Our Current Age

Today in the postmodern age, Christianity is being challenged
as to its right or ability to influence the moral issues of our
day. The directive of "separation of church and state" that is
imposed by our government promotes secularism as a controlling
principle of American life. This has contributed greatly to the
deterioration of moral values and the unrestrained evil that we
are experiencing today. Interestingly, the Bible predicts such
times as these.

But know this, that in the last days perilous times will come: For men will be lovers of themselves, lovers of money, boasters, proud, blasphemers, disobedient to parents, unthankful, unholy, unloving, unforgiving, slanderers, without self-control, brutal despisers of good, traitors, headstrong, haughty, lovers of pleasure rather than lovers of God, having a form of godliness bur denying its power. And from such people turn away! (2 Tim. 3:1–5)

The pressing question that presents itself throughout history is, Is there any hope for our world? Yes! We desperately need to believe in and pray for a spiritual revival in these last days that will influence all facets of society, thus revealing the invisible hand of God in the glove of history, controlling and steering history by His providence. Encouraging admonition comes from the late Oswald Chambers:

"Let the past sleep, but let it sleep on the bosom of Christ. Leave the irreparable past in His hands, and step out into the irresistible future with Him"

(My Utmost for His Highest (1956) section Dec.31)

Biblical Foundation for Understanding Time, History, and Eternity

There are many theories about how we understand the flow of history. It is important to know what constitutes the actual flow of history in order that we may clarify the significance of historical events. I espouse the view that I believe most adequately explains the development of secular and biblical history—namely, the linear and providential view of history.

The Linear View of History

History (as contemporarily understood by Western thought) tends to follow an assumption of linear progression: "This happened and then that happened; that happened because this happened first." It's the whole idea of cause and effect. This helps us see how historical events connect with one another, resulting in an understanding of the flow and purpose of life. History has a beginning and an ending.

The Providential View of History

This is the Christian view of history that is meaningful in the sense that it is moving toward a distinct goal. The idea is that providence is the continued exercise of God the creator, preserving and governing all that takes place in the world and directing all things to their appointed end.

God is the first cause of creation and developing history. It is important that we understand biblical history as true history, not composed myth. Because of this I believe there is still hope for a revival of Christianity to take place in America and around the world. I am using the term *revival* in the broad sense as referring to God in His sovereignty and providence intervening in world events, resulting in directing the course of history toward His eternal purposes. These changes are considered in Christianity as the revival or renewal of the moral and spiritual principles needed to preserve culture and societies. A study of Biblical history reveals events that have brought great changes to countries, communities, and personal lives.

More importantly, God's intervention allows for continual change and blessing to take place in the future. In Christianity there has always been an optimistic view that God has been working and continues to work in and for His creation. My purpose is to highlight interventions of God's hand that took place in various historical and spiritual events and reveal His desire for future generations to know that God is for us. Many of these interventions were present but suppressed and inactive in the culture and the people of its day. However, circumstances developed that allowed these to be revived and become active in awakening the culture and its people to the presence of God.

> "God is always working and we need to find where He is working and join Him in the work!" (Blackaby, *Experiencing God* 1990, 49)

A popular song of some time ago suggests, "What the world needs now is love, sweet love. It's the only thing there's just too little of, not just for some but for everyone" (Warwick 1967). This is certainty true today. Why doesn't the world recognize God's love? As we witness so much violence and turmoil in our world, it has caused many to question God. Is there any source of love available? Yes! God is still the only source of genuine love. The most powerful expressions of God's love and concern are found in the gospel of John and in 2 Corinthians, which reveals God's heart and desire for all humanity.

> For God so loved the world that He gave His only begotten Son, that whoever believes in Him should not perish but have everlasting life. For God did not send His son into the world to condemn the world, but that world through him might be saved. (John 3:16–17)

> And this is the condemnation, that the light has come into the world, and men loved darkness rather than light, because their deeds were evil. But he who does the truth comes to the light, that his deeds may be clearly seen, that they have been done in God. (John 3:19–21)

But even if our gospel is veiled, it is veiled to those who are perishing, whose minds the god of this age has blinded, who do not believe, lest the light of the gospel of the glory of Christ, who is the image of God, should shine on them. (2 Cor. 4:3–4)

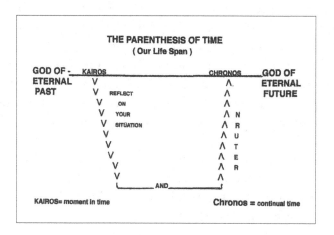

We need an awakening to the truth that this world is temporary and we are living inside the parentheses of time between God's action in the past and God's promised action in the future. God is Lord over time. He creates *kairos* moments in the continuing *chronos* of time for us to reflect on our present situations and adjust our lives with God. Then we continue in the chronos of time.

He has created the parentheses for each of us to bring our lives unto His salvation so that we may enter that eternal future, which is His heaven.

We do not know how long each of our parentheses may last, so it is imperative that we act as soon as possible. God has not forsaken the world, but we have forsaken Him. The Bible is full of incidents that reveal that God is for us in spite of the turmoil surrounding us and in spite of our turning away from Him. Take heart—God is constantly intervening in history and will continue to do so until He brings all things into His eternal purpose.

As we proceed to explore God's continuous action in the world as seen in the scriptures, may we be encouraged that He is in control, not us or the world's leaders. May our hearts be stimulated by the fact that God is for us and for every human being on the face of the earth in spite of our circumstances. I will highlight selected periods of biblical history beginning with the book of Genesis and proceeding through the Old and the New Testaments, revealing how God's intervening hand directed the course of biblical events toward His will and purpose. That purpose will make it evident that God is for us, giving us confidence that, regardless of the situation, He is in control.

> Fear not, for I am with you; Be not dismayed, for I am your God. I will strengthen you, Yes, I will help you, I will uphold you with My righteous right hand. (Isa. 41:10)

> Peace I leave with you, My peace I give to you; not as the world gives do I give to you. Let not your heart be troubled, neither let it be afraid. (John 14:27)

Reflecting on One of My Kairos Moments

During World War II, I decided to join the navy. I had to get my mother's permission since I was only seventeen years old. She consented because she believed I lacked maturity and thought the service would make a man out of me. I quickly went to the recruiting office along with my boyhood friend Roger Whipple. We were both excited about our possible adventure. Arriving at the recruiting center, we enrolled with great enthusiasm. As we were being processed, a marine officer came in and announced that he needed several more men to complete his unit. Thus, he proceeded to choose several men from those standing in line, and to my dismay, my buddy was chosen for the marines. He was eventually shipped to the Pacific and was killed at the Battle of Iwo Jima. I, however, was assigned to boot camp in Sampson, New York.

While waiting for my assignment there, I had a few days liberty. I decided to take time to visit my mother in Massachusetts by train; however, the trip would go beyond my liberty zone. I took a chance anyway. When I returned to the base, the Navy Patrol arrested me for being AWOL and escorted me to my chief officer, who informed me that my original company had shipped out so he was assigning me to another company, which eventually was assigned to the Caribbean area to serve on a ship repair barge. This was a kairos moment in my life, and I eventually came to see that God was for me and was directing my future. My original company was assigned to the Pacific front, where the heaviest fighting was going on, and I lost contact with them. Looking back, I now know that God was directing my life for His will and purpose. When certain things confuse you, consider that it may be a kairos moment. God is always involved in our lives.

God's Directives through History

As the world's story developed through the centuries, the hand of God appeared as if it were in a glove, directing and controlling historical events by His providential will. That is, God was orchestrating events to conform to His eternal purpose for humankind. Biblical history runs parallel to world history, accomplishing His eternal will. Unfortunately, many in the world are not aware of this and generally have a fatalistic or flawed view of the future. I am not doing an exhaustive study of the many events recorded in the Old Testament, New Testament, or accompanying history. I have chosen some major events from the scriptures that reveal God's messianic plan begun in Genesis, unfolded in the Gospels, and culminating in the promises of Revelation. God has always had an eye toward the redemption of His world.

Consider the Unconditional Love of God

The very nature of God is love. Much has been written about the character of God, and many agree that His most endearing trait is that He is love. Love is not something God chooses to do or give. It is the essence of who He is. He doesn't just love; He *is* love. It motivates His every action, directs His activities, and reflects His desires. The focus of God's love is redemption. God's unconditional and intense love for fallen humanity motivated the plan of salvation. God is for us and seeks to make us whole and complete. It goes back to the state of Adam when God breathed life into him and made him a living soul. This life gives us the capacity and desire to be in relationship with God. To live in God is to live in love.

One of Karl Barth's students asked him to share the most significant theological truth he had discovered in all his years of study. Barth, one of the most prolific theologians of the twentieth century who wrote many commentaries and theological studies, thought for a moment, smiled, and said, "Jesus loves me, this I know for the Bible tells me so."

> Who shall separate us from the love of Christ? Shall tribulation, or distress, or persecution, or famine, or nakedness or peril or sword? ... Yet in all these things we are more than conquerors through Him who loved us. For I am persuaded that neither death nor life, nor angels, nor principalities, nor powers, nor things present nor things to come, nor height, nor depth, nor any other created thing, shall be able to separate us from the love of God which is in Christ Jesus our Lord. (Rom. 8:35, 37–39)

Part 1

Evidence That God Is for Us in the Old Testament

Chapter 1

The Creation and Fall, the Flood, and the Tower of Babel

The biblical account of creation is vastly different from that of its Near Eastern counterparts. Man is the apex of God's creation, made in God's image and made steward of His earth (Gen. 1:28). This creation was prepared with man in mind for his use and enjoyment (Gen. 1:29–30). Although he was also created to worship his Creator, it was not a wearisome task.

Historiography of the Scriptures

> The Biblical authors had a worldview by which history was viewed as linear. The past, present, and future all had importance.... The Biblical writers considered all phases of time as important. There is virtually no understanding of history in the modern sense among cultures of the ancient Near Eastern view of history was cyclical and assigned little importance to the past or to the future. (Bryant)

I agree with these observations and believe they serve as sufficient evidence that the Bible is not a product of mythology. My goal is to observe selected historical settings of God's people as furnished by both the Old and New Testament. Christianity was not born in a vacuum. God has been working among the peoples of the world, especially Israel, since before Christ came. Kevin DeYoung, pastor of the University Reformed Church, wrote,

> The story of the Old Testament is nothing if not a story of divine providence. On every page, in every promise, behind every prophecy, is the sure hand of God. He sustains all things, directs all things, plans all things, ordains all things, superintends all the counsel of His will. **(TheGospelCoalition.org, accessed 2018)**

The dynamic story of the Old Testament begins with the creation account: "In the beginning God created." But unfortunately, it wasn't long before His action had to move toward redemption. God created humans—male and female—in His own image. Adam and Eve enjoyed the intimacy of God and unbroken fellowship. However, they chose to disobey God's prohibition not to eat of the tree of the knowledge of good and evil. Adam, through the urging of his wife, Eve, who was deceived by Satan in the decision, lost their fellowship with their Creator. But God's hand was extended toward the work of restoration immediately. As Adam and Eve became self-conscious and tried to cover their nakedness with fig leaves, God provided clothing from an animal skin. This act of providing clothing revealed God's ultimate plan of redemption and restoration, introducing a future sacrificial system. The first sacrifice pointed toward the ultimate sacrificial Lamb of God, Jesus Himself.

In Genesis 3:15, the promise is given that the seed of a woman would someday crush the serpent's head (Satan), playing a part in undoing the effects of the fall. We discover that the seed of woman is Jesus, who was born of the Virgin Mary, fulfilling the prophecy of Isaiah 7:14: "The virgin shall conceive and bear a Son, and shall call His name Immanuel." *Immanuel* means "God with us." Also, see the fulfillment in Matthew 1:20–23.

The life and ministry of Jesus Christ introduced the kingdom of God and its power. And in His death on the cross, He crushed Satan's power. By His resurrection, He guaranteed eternal life at the end of the world. This is a monumental example of God's hand in securing salvation for all humankind. Though Adam and Eve were expelled from the garden, they would continue to live and bear children. But they would live under the curse of unyielding ground and painful childbirth.

The Birth and Life of Cain and Abel (Gen. 4:1–26)

Abel was a keeper of sheep, while Cain was a tiller of the ground. After some time, Cain brought an offering of fruit to the Lord, while Abel brought the firstborn of his flock. The Lord respected Abel and his offering, but He did not respect Cain's offering. And Cain was angry (Gen. 4:3–5). God tried to explain to him that if he would have followed what God required of him and not allowed sin to take over by his act of disobedience, he too would have been accepted (Gen. 4:6–7). Cain and his brother were out in the field together when Cain attacked Abel and killed him (Gen. 4:8). God came along and confronted Cain by saying, "Where is Abel, your brother?" Cain answered, "I do not know. Am I my brother's keeper?" God then reproached Cain. "What have you done? The voice of your brother's blood cries out to Me from the ground." The blood cried out for vengeance and judgment. Cain would be a fugitive on the earth, and though he tilled the soil, it would not yield its strength (Gen. 4:9–12). Cain was fearful that if others found him, they would kill him, but God set a mark on him so that no one could kill him (Gen. 4:13–15). Oh, the mercy of God extended to humankind!

Even in this tragic event, God revealed His determination to be for us in every situation. In Genesis 4:17, Cain and his wife birthed Enoch. It appears that Cain promised himself a new beginning in life through Enoch. In the meantime, Adam and Eve had a son named Seth, and in verses 25–26, Eve says, "For God has appointed another seed for me instead of Abel, whom Cain killed." Seth too had a son, Enosh. Unfortunately, as humankind developed, God saw that their wickedness was multiplying upon the earth and that every intent of their hearts was evil continually (Gen. 4:6:5). And the Lord was sorry that He had made humans; it grieved His heart (Gen. 4:6:6).

It is tragic to note that a sinful act of disobedience in the garden of Eden carried over to the next generation of human beings, displaying the seeds of evil that came from within humankind. It also reveals that in spite of this disobedience, God is not finished with His will and desire. From the beginning, God revealed that He was still for us and will continue to be for us throughout history. Even with the tragic incident of Cain murdering his brother Abel, the first murder, God did not give up on His creation.

Noah and the Flood

God determined to wipe out humankind and all creatures on the face of the earth. I believe God was sorely grieved that He had to take this action. However, a man named Noah found grace in the eyes of the Lord. Here was a just man. God decided that through him, He would continue to fulfill His desire to have a people again. So He made a covenant with Noah. Noah built an ark, as instructed by God, to save himself, his family, and some animals from the flood that God was sending as His judgment upon that generation.

When the flood abated, He restored the world through Noah's sons: Ham, Shem, and Japheth (Gen. 6:9–22, 10:1–32).

- *Ham:* Cush, Mizraim, Put, and Canaan (Africa and Arabia)
- *Shem:* Elam, Asshur, Arphaxad, Lud, and Aram (Hebrew and Assyria)
- *Japheth:* Gomer, Magog, Madai, Javan, Tubal, Meshech, and Tiras (Asia Minor Europe)

God's love for humanity is strong. He desires to have a people possessing His eternal life. This is still true today and for the future.

The Tower of Babel: The Attempt to Divert God's Plan

> Now the whole earth had one language and one speech. And it came to pass, as they journeyed from the east, that they found a plain in the land of Shinar, and they dwelt there. Then they said to one another, "Come, let us make bricks and bake them thoroughly." They had bricks for stone, and they had asphalt for mortar. And they said, "Come, let us build ourselves a city and a tower whose top is in the heavens; let us make a name for ourselves, lest we be scattered abroad over the face of the whole earth." (Gen. 11:1–4)

God's intent for the nations was for people to spread across the earth and not to congregate in one place. In the beginning, God told humankind to be "fruitful and multiply, and fill the earth" (Gen. 1:28, 9:1) because He wanted the whole world populated with His image bearers (Gen. 1:26–27). Think what it must have been like for a family to leave the area of Babel and go out on their own. They had to look for a suitable place to live. Once they found it, they subsisted by hunting and gathering and living in crude dwellings or caves until they could support themselves through agriculture and taking advantage of natural resources. Families multiplied rapidly and developed their own languages and cultures and their own distinctive physical characteristics influenced by their environments. As the populations of the groups grew larger, the changes stabilized and became more or less permanent.

God intervenes when it is necessary to accomplish His will and purpose for humankind (Gen. 11:5–9). Therefore, we can witness that, from the beginning of time, God is definitely for us, and we can trust He will continue to be with us throughout all history. We are wanderers and sojourners in the world, separated from God, our Creator. But God has made a way back to Himself. He has provided signposts along the way. Through His Word, His hand is pointing the way to His help. The Word of God is progressively revealing that God is for us and that He desires to fortify our lives with hope and assurance in these troubled times. Be assured and take heart that God is in control and will accomplish His eternal purpose in the world and for eternity.

Chapter 2

The Patriarchs: Abraham, Isaac, Jacob, and Joseph
(Gen. 11:10–32, 12–50)

The genealogies of this section serve as a transitional link from the primeval period of humans to the patriarchal period, whereby God continues to unfold His ultimate redemptive plan. In Genesis 10, we saw how the families of the earth came from Noah's three sons: Japheth, Ham, and Shem. The descendants of Japheth became the Indo-European people who settled in parts of Asia Minor, north into Europe and westward to Spain. The descendants of Ham moved into North Africa and the East (Arabia). The descendants of Shem, Noah's firstborn son, became the Semitic peoples. The line of faith in God came through Shem and his descendants. *The key person was Shem, who leads us to Abram (who later becomes Abraham).*

It's Abraham's seed that clearly follows God's action toward the New Testament coming of the Messiah. As we will see, God is always working in history for humankind's future good and eventually for eternal life that includes you and me. *The key factor as we move to the period of Abraham is the important idea of covenant.* It is essential for us to understand that it is through covenant that God determined to reveal His eternal love for humankind. The goal of God's love is relationship, and our relationship with God is an intimate one. To know God intimately brings change of behavior, desires, and security. A covenant is between two parties, both promising to adhere to the demands set down by the covenant. The question is whether we can keep our end of the bargain. Hopefully yes! *Again, realize that this particular period is very important in our thesis that God is for us.* Now, God begins to make humans better, and He starts as He always starts—with a person who will do His will, even if he or she does not do His will perfectly. The patriarch constitutes the head of a tribe or family. The term usually refers to the Israelite forefathers Abraham, Isaac, and Jacob. In keeping with the purpose for this book, to reveal God's hand in historic events, I would like to point out that the witness arising out of the patriarchal period is the very important principle: *God's hand is exercised through His covenant.* The key people in this period would keep the promise of the Messiah alive from generation to generation until the Messiah was revealed. The Messianic line extends from Adam through Seth to Noah and his sons (Gen. 5), from Noah through Shem to Abram (Gen. 11:10–27). As we follow the line of Abram, we discover how he reveals that *God is for us and future generations because of God's covenant with Abraham.*

Covenants: The Backbone of the Bible

Think about why God extended His love to all generations as demonstrated through the development of the covenant. It is because of His unshakable commitment to His creation and to the humans He created. The point I am trying to make here is that God loves what He created; He is committed to what He loves! So, when man rebelled and rejected God's ways, breaking His covenant, He brought the great flood during Noah's time, though it grieved His heart to have to do so. He preserved Noah and his family with the determination to continue to have a people after His own heart following the great flood. God made a covenant with Noah and his family: "I now establish my covenant with you and with your descendants after you...Never again will all life be cut off by the waters of a flood." (Gen. 9:9–11). The implication of the statement "your descendants after you" points to Abraham and his progeny and the future establishment of the Messianic covenant. The repopulation of the earth began with Noah's sons Japheth, Ham, and Shem.

God's Hand in the Call of Abraham (Gen. 12:1–9)

Once again we witness God's hand in history, moving it forward toward His ultimate purpose for humankind. We take history for granted and presume that people everywhere have always seen that there is some kind of meaning or purpose in events.

> By faith Abraham obeyed when he was called to go out to the place which he would receive as an inheritance. And he went out, not knowing where he was going. (**Heb. 11:8**)

With the twelfth chapter of Genesis, we enter a new era in Bible history. The scriptures make no attempt to report the history of the entire human race. They give much more attention to God's providential work in certain people and circumstances to accomplish His eternal purpose within historical events. In Abram's covenant with God, is there any doubt that God's hand was in history pursuing His eternal purpose? God made some incredible promises to Abram and his seed (offspring). A promise of land for an everlasting possession, an innumerable family, and blessings on all nations of the earth.

> I will make you a great nation; I will bless you, and make your name great; And you shall be a blessing. I will bless those who bless you, and I will curse him who curses you. *And in you all*

the families of the earth shall be blessed. (Gen. 12:2–3, emphasis added)

The greatest promise is expressed in the New Testament by the apostle Paul in his epistle to the Galatians when he states,

Now to Abraham and his seed were the promises made. He does not say, "And to seeds," as of many, but as of one, "and to your Seed," who is Christ." (Gal. 3:16)

My purpose is not to expound all the epochs dealing with the patriarchal family but simply to view those significant things that help us to see God's continuing hand of providence on them. There is an important event that we observe about the fulfillment of these promises. Abraham's wife, Sarah, was barren and had no children (Gen. 16). The repetition of barrenness emphasizes that God's promise to Abraham for descendants would not be fulfilled through natural means. Consider the fact that Sarah was barren and was very old yet still bore a son. Abraham's descendants are the result of God's hand in a special creation, for they were born from barren wombs. This is God's action bringing lasting results for future generations, which includes you and me today.

The Abrahamic covenant becomes a lasting principle for the future of humankind. Sarah rejoiced in the son of promise, Isaac, but she died before Isaac was married and fathered children. But God's promises never die. Abraham buried Sarah in the cave of the field at Machpelah in the land of Canaan. So the field and the cave were deeded over to Abraham by the sons of Heth for a burial site (Gen. 23:19–20).

In spite of Sarah's death and burial, God's promise to establish the land of Canaan as a perpetual possession was being fulfilled. Abraham now turned his concern to Isaac to find him a wife. He was aware that in order for the covenant from God to continue through Isaac, he must have a wife and descendants who would continue the covenant.

God's Hand of Providence in Choosing a Bride for Isaac (Gen. 24)

Abraham was determined that Isaac should not choose a wife from the godless women in Canaan, so He sent his trusted servant to Mesopotamia to find a bride for Isaac (Gen. 24:1–9). As the servant went on the mission of seeking a bride for Isaac, he met a woman, Rebekah, at a well. Note that the servant prayed that God would give a sign: the woman who comes for water and offers him a drink as well as one for his camels would be the bride God had chosen (Gen. 24:10–14). Before he had finished praying, Rebekah arrived with a jar on her shoulder. The servant hurried to meet her and asked for a drink from her jar. She not only gave him a drink but offered to draw water for his camels. The servant was invited into the house of Bethuel, the father of Rebekah, and stated his mission to her father, Laban, and her brother (Gen. 24:34–49). They granted permission for Rebekah to go and become the bride of Isaac (Gen. 24:50–60). There are a couple of factors to note from this account; the providence and leading of the Lord in all the details in this chapter is obvious.

1. The straightforward manner in which Rebekah made her decision to go with this servant and become the bride of Isaac is impressive (see Gen. 24:58). No doubt her father, Bethuel, sensed this was ordered of God.
2. The servant's prayer indicates that he was aware that the choice needed to be made according to God's will and not Abraham's desire or approval alone.

God's Covenant Passed On (Gen. 25:19–26)

Isaac and Rebekah had been married for twenty years before the birth of their sons, Jacob and Esau. They may have remained childless due to Rebekah's barrenness had not the Lord answered their prayers. God is still in control by His covenant purposes, even though many situations arise that threaten His plan. Dr. David Jeremiah, in his book *Heroes of the Faith*, states,

> Isaac was concerned about the future and continuation of the promises made to Abraham. He was alert to his responsibility to pass on the blessing he himself received.

Let us summarize God's actions through these patriarchs. God ordained whom He would create as a chosen people who would eventually birth the promised Messiah. The chosen line was passed on to Abraham's son Isaac and then to his son Jacob. God changed Jacob's name to Israel, and his twelve sons became the twelve tribes of Israel.

God's Hand of Providence in the Life of Joseph (Gen. 37–50)

The life of Joseph covers a large portion of the latter part of Genesis (37:1–50:26). We would be remiss to overlook the significance of Joseph in continuing God's covenant to the future generations. Jacob's sons were angered by their father's favoritism of their younger brother Joseph. Their evil deed against Joseph, though not justifiable, was very cruel. But God's hand of providence was watching over Joseph's destiny and his role in the future of history. Let us take note of the various scenarios concerning Joseph's plight and witness God's involvement toward directing His eternal purpose. Joseph's dreams increased the family's hatred toward Him. These dreams were certainly not ordinary dreams, but they appeared to suggest that Joseph was being directed by the providence of God. Jacob may have suspected that God was directing Joseph's destiny because it reminded him of his wrestling with a man that turned out to be God and resulted in his name being changed to Israel (meaning "he struggled with God"). Now Joseph's father kept the matter in mind (Gen. 37:10); however, his brothers were jealous and angry and eventually plotted to kill him (Gen. 37:18). In His sovereignty, God eventually had Joseph sent to Egypt through this despicable act on the part of his brothers. Rather than killing him, they sold him to traveling Midianite merchants. However, the Midianites sold Joseph for twenty shekels of silver to Ishmaelites, who took him to Egypt (Gen. 37:28). There, he was sold to Potiphar, one of Pharoah's officials. A very interesting statement appears in Joseph's experience: "The LORD was with Joseph." And he prospered in the house of his master. Potiphar put him in charge of his entire household. Eventually, Potiphar's wife became enamored with Joseph and tried to seduce him, but he resisted and reminded her that her husband did not include her as part of his duties. He declared that he could not do such a wicked thing against God. She insisted on seducing him, even trying to force him to her bed. As he pulled away, she grabbed his cloak. She immediately called her household servants, accusing Joseph of misbehavior. When Potiphar heard of this incident, he burned with anger and put Joseph in prison. Even though Joseph experienced enslavement, unfair accusations, and imprisonment, God's hand intervened during this time, giving Joseph the ability to interpret the dreams of two fellow prisoners, Pharaoh's cupbearer and baker. Sometime after this, the cupbearer, who had been released, discovered that Pharaoh experienced a dream that no one could interpret, and he remembered Joseph's ability to interpret his dream two years earlier and notified Pharaoh. Immediately, Joseph was taken from the prison and, after being made presentable, brought before Pharaoh. He interpreted his dream but not before making Pharaoh aware that the interpretation came from God. This resulted in Pharaoh's putting Joseph in charge of the whole land of Egypt with great authority (see Gen. 40–41). How can one not see the providence of God in Joseph's life? All of this eventually resulted in Joseph's saving Jacob and his family from a devastating famine and restored his relationship with his brothers. Joseph's life displayed integrity and forgiveness. He and his family stayed in Egypt and saw the birth of his third generation. At the time of his death, he encouraged them by saying that God would come to their aid when needed, based on His oath to Abraham, Isaac, and Jacob. Unfortunately, a new pharaoh arose who did not know Joseph, and Israel was put in harsh slavery for many years. Their hardships under Pharaoh caused them to desire deliverance. Notice how God's sovereign hand is stretched forth in this total situation to direct His plan and purpose. God raised up Moses to be the deliverer for His people, Israel. God did not intend to keep Israel in bondage but to move them forward toward Canaan and their future as a nation serving His divine providence.

Chapter 3

Moses: God's Instrument to Reveal God Is for Us

There is a very interesting summary in the New Testament of Moses's experience in leading Israel, written in Acts 7:1–60 by Stephen when he was accused of blasphemy and brought before the Sanhedrin. Stephen confronted the Jewish Sanhedrin with his bold speech that led to his death. He compared their treatment of Jesus with the earlier rejection of God's messengers such as Joseph, Moses, and the prophets. Stephen said,

> This Moses whom they rejected saying, "Who made you a ruler and a judge?" is the one God sent to be a ruler and a deliverer by hand of the Angel who appeared to him in the bush. (Acts 7:35)

The life and ministry of Moses certainly demonstrates God's desire to encourage His world that He is for us. God was aware of the difficulties of His people and, never forgetting His covenant, promised to restore them to their own land. The covenant was not made with Israel because they were righteous. It was made because God is righteous and the nations were evil. God honored His promises to Israel, and He will honor His promises to us as well. Moses, being called of God, delivered Israel out of Egypt's slavery by a divine, supernatural, powerful hand, creating devastating plagues against Egypt and stubborn

Pharaoh, even to the plague of death upon the firstborn. God told Moses how He intended to bring Israel's deliverance. Note several phrases God uses:

> For with a strong hand he will let them go, and with a strong hand he will drive them out of his land. "I am the LORD, I appeared to Abraham, to Isaac, and to Jacob as God almighty. I have also established my covenant with them to give them the land of Canaan, the land of their pilgrimage, in which they were strangers. And I have also heard the groaning of the children of Israel whom the Egyptians keep in bondage and I have remembered My covenant. I am the LORD; I will bring you out from under the burdens of the Egyptians, I will rescue you from their bondage, and I will redeem you with an outstretched arm and with great judgments. I will take you as my people, and I will be your God. Then you shall know that I am the LORD your God.... And I bring you to the land which I swore to give Abraham, to Isaac, to Jacob. (Exo. 6:1–8)

We do not want to underestimate the importance of the life of Moses. Moses was a great leader, law-giver, prophet, and judge of Israel. God declared ownership of Israel. They no longer belonged to Pharaoh but to God (Exo. 13:1–16). Their predicament was not an accident. Exodus 13:18 says, "So God led the people ... to the Red Sea." He knew they needed the Red Sea experience, and their upcoming journey, to learn some things from Him. Those who follow the guidance of God are not free from trials and perils. Our journey may seem long and trials great, but God is faithful and always for us throughout our journey.

No temptation has overtaken you except such as
is common to man; but God is faithful, who will
not allow you to be tempted beyond what you are
able, but with the temptation will also make the
way of escape, that you may be able to bear it. (1
Cor. 10:13)

The Israelites' trek through the wilderness toward Canaan
was a great disappointment since Moses was not allowed to enter.
However, he trained Joshua to take charge to fulfill God's covenant
promise. Moses is the most significant figure in the Old Testament,
revealing God's purpose and covenant of love. Is there any doubt
that God Almighty is for us in every generation, even ours?

Joshua Fulfills the Promise of Israel Conquering Canaan (Deut. 34)

The long and tedious journey through the wilderness under
Moses's leadership produced the tabernacle for worship and
the Ten Commandments and other laws. Unfortunately, the
people strained against these things as well as Moses's leadership
and Aaron's priesthood, and eventually many people died in
the wilderness. However, the book of Deuteronomy reveals the
determination on the part of Moses, under God, to reinstate
these things to the next generation. Moses was not allowed to
enter Canaan (see Deut. 32). He was ordered by God to go to the
top of Mount Nebo, where he could view the land. Moses died
and was buried by the Lord in an unmarked grave (Deut. 34).
What would the Israelites do now? They had come all this way,
they were a new generation, and their leader was gone. However,
God is not dead! He immediately spoke to Joshua in 1:2–3.

Moses My servant is dead. Now therefore, arise,
go over this Jordan, you and all this people, to the

land which I am giving to them—the children
of Israel. Every place that the sole of your foot
will tread upon I have given to you, as I said to
Moses.

Here again we see God's hand continuing His ultimate
covenant purpose of moving history to its glorious end. God
moved His hand to anoint Joshua for the task of conquering the
land of Canaan. We will observe how God's intervening hand
moves to accomplish the various victories of conquest. Note how
God aided Joshua with the various events he engaged in:

1. *Rahab and the spies (Gen. 2:8–11).* Rahab said, "I know
   that the LORD has given this land to you and great fear
   of youths befallen us.... We have heard how the LORD
   dried up the water of the Red Sea.... When we heard
   of it, our hearts melted and everyone's courage failed
   because of you for the LORD your God is in the heaven
   above and of the earth below."
2. *Crossing the Jordan River (3:13–17).* The priests who
   carried the ark, which symbolized the presence of God,
   were to carry it to the edge of the river and as soon
   as their feet touched the water, the upstream stopped
   flowing and piled up in a heap a great distance away.
   The people crossed over it opposite Jericho. The priests
   who carried the ark of the covenant of the Lord stood
   firm on dry ground. How could we fail to recognize the
   presence of God in this miracle?
3. *The Fall of Jericho (5:13–6:27).* This is probably the most
   familiar miracle known to most readers of the Bible. It is
   obvious that the dramatic circling of the walls, the sound
   of the trumpets, and the shouting of the people did not
   accomplish the crumbling of the walls. It was the very
   presence and power of God, along with the courage of
   the people.

4. *The sun stood still (10:1–14).* This miracle has been debated through the years because it involves the altering of the universe itself. My question simply is this: Why is it impossible for our creating God to do this? It's His universe! Some other explanations are that it was a total eclipse or that the biblical account is a poetic interpretation because the book of Asher is an ancient poetic and in Habakkuk 3:10–11, the prophet uses the language of the sun and moon standing still to describe the awesomeness of Yahweh's appearance. But the details of the account clearly reveal that this poetic description of how God helped His people was fulfilled literally that day. However, "the most commonly accepted explanation is that God miraculously allowed light on that day to be extended, giving a full day of light. It was the result of supernatural intervention by the creator of the universe" (David Jeremiah's Bible, notes, 291).

I think there is sufficient evidence that the hand of God was extended to help Joshua conquer Canaan and establish Israel in the land. The death of Joshua eventually created a difficult situation for Israel. God had fulfilled His promise to the patriarchs by giving the land to Israel. Joshua's farewell speech before his death reminds them of all that had transpired in capturing Canaan and giving them rest and that it was all accomplished by God, not Joshua. It was His intervening hand that was continuing to lead them now and in the future (read Joshua 23 and 24). Joshua, before his death, admonished Israel to keep their covenant relationship. It was very important for God to be able to intervene for them in a time of need. Sadly, as we will see, the book of Judges records their disobedience to God's covenant. We should never take His covenant lightly. We always need to keep in mind that every generation is only one generation away from losing their godly heritage by forgetting their commitment. It is amazing to me how patient God is with us. His love for His creation and people should be a revelation to us when we focus upon God's wrath. If we learn nothing else in this study, we should learn that God so loved the world that He committed His Son Jesus to come to this earth and humble Himself in order to reveal God the Father's love and commitment to save the human race for His honor and glory to be displayed ultimately in heaven. But remember, it took the sacrificial death of Jesus and His resurrection to solidify the Father's covenant that establishes our eternity in heaven. So let us not lose heart when we witness the attitude of humanity such as we see in the time of the Judges. On the surface it appears that all is lost. But remember, God never changes His mind about His love and the covenant He made with us. God is for us throughout the ages to come.

Chapter 4

God's Providence Revealed in Judges and Ruth

These books also demonstrate how God is constantly revealing His love and concern for us and His divine purpose. The books of Judges and Ruth are certainly a challenge to our premise of God's continued presence in humankind's journey. Nevertheless, He reveals His active love and patience throughout both.

The Book of Judges

The book of Judges forms a bridge between the conquest of the promised land of Canaan under the leadership of Joshua and the later establishment of the monarchy under Saul, David, and Solomon. Judges is a tragic account of how God was taken for granted and betrayed by His children year after year, century after century. It is a sad contrast to the book of Joshua, which chronicles the blessings God bestowed on the Israelites for their obedience in conquering the land. In Judges, they were disobedient and idolatrous, leading to their many defeats and subjugation. Yet God has never failed to open His arms in love to His people whenever they repent from their wicked ways and call on His name.

The Period of the Judges

> And when the Lord raised up Judges for them, the LORD was with the judge and delivered them out of the hand of their enemies all the days of the judge (Judges 2:18)

> When all that generation had been gathered to their fathers, another generation arose after them who did not know the LORD nor the work He had done for Israel. Then the children of Israel did evil in the sight of the LORD, and served the Baals.... Wherever they went out, the hand of the LORD was against them for calamity, as the LORD had said, and the LORD had sworn to them. And they were greatly distressed. (Judges 2:10–11, 15)

The book of Judges depicts Israel's covenant apostasy and the resulting oppression at the hands of their neighbors (Judges 2:6–7, 2:10–15). It is obvious that evil powers are constantly operating to foil God's ultimate eternal plan for His kingdom. It seems that every new generation brings change and challenge to God's purpose. The hand of the Lord works both ways, for and against situations. Will we see God's hand extended in this situation? The book is clear that the fault lay in Israel's sin and not God's failure to keep His covenant promises. God is long-suffering and merciful. This is evident in the fact that He raised up judges to deliver His people in spite of their ignoring Him and worshiping the gods of Canaan (Judges 2:2–3, 10–14, 20–21). The judges or saviors indicate that the hand of God was still actively keeping His side of the covenant relationship. These judges were not trained arbiters of legal cases like the judges of today. They were spirit-endowed leaders chosen by God for specific tasks (see Judges 3:9–10; 6:34; 11:29; 13:25).

The List of Judges

The judges were as follows:

- Othniel (Judges 3:7–11): Nephew of Caleb; delivered Israel from Mesopotamia
- Ehud (Judges 3:12–30): Left handed; killed Eglon, king of Moab
- Jephthah (Judges 11:1–12:7): A harlot's son who defeated the Amonites
- Gideon (Judges 6:11–8:35): Led three hundred Israelites to defeat an army of Midianites
- Samson (Judges 13:1–16:31): Delivered the Israelites from the Philistines
- Deborah (Judges 4:1–5:3): Urged Barak to attack the army of Canaanites

Judges about whom fewer details are given are Tola (Judges 10:1–2), Jair (Judges 10:3–5), Elon (Judges 12:11–12), and Abdon (Judges 12:13–15). These are not in chronological order.

> And when the Lord raised up Judges for them, the Lord was with the judge and delivered them out of the hand of their enemies all the days of the judge; for the LORD was moved with pity by their groaning because of those who oppressed them and harassed them. (Judges 2:18)

One of the key factors in the time of the judges is the concluding statement in Judges 21:25: "In those days of Israel there was no king in Israel; everyone did what was right in his own eyes."

It was only the hand of God directing them by fulfilling His part of the covenant that preserved Israel. God is determined to carry out His promises to humankind to the end of the age.

The turmoil throughout Judges could not override His eternal purpose. Judges is a testament of God's faithfulness. God is moving constantly to keep His purpose alive for each generation; otherwise, He would have destroyed His people completely. We can be assured that His covenant with us to have eternal life will be fulfilled. Again, note that God is for us in every era.

The Book of Ruth: A Shining Light in Dark Times

I would be remiss if I did not include the book of Ruth, the events of which transpired during the time of the Judges. The book, to some degree, becomes a shining light in the midst of the events described in Judges. It reminds us that, regardless of our dark circumstances, God's hand is always present and working. The book has been attributed to the prophet Samuel as the possible author. This is certainly feasible since he was instrumental, under God's direction, in seeking a king for Israel. Ruth is a majestic story of God's providence. It appears that God's hand fell hard upon Naomi and her family (Ruth 1). Famine in Judah forced the family of Elimelech to move from Bethlehem to Moab. Elimelech was accompanied by Naomi, his wife, and their sons, Mahlon and Kilion. Elimelech died, leaving Naomi to care for herself and their sons. The sons ended up marrying Moabite women, Ruth and Orpah. Unfortunately, the two sons also died, leaving the Moabite widows without the security of a husband or sons. Calamity after calamity caused Naomi to say, "The hand of the LORD has gone out against me.... The Almighty has dealt very bitterly with me" (Ruth 1:13, 20). It's telling that we frequently assign our plights to God's action against us and not to our own actions and bad decisions. Little did Naomi realize that God's hand was leading her to a bountiful future. After living in Moab for ten years and now without a husband or sons and two daughters-in-law to care for, Naomi was deeply troubled. Both Mahlon and Kilion died, leaving her without her sons and her husband. Hearing of available food in Bethlehem, she decided to return there. She was, however, concerned about her widowed daughters-in-law, Ruth and Orpah, and insisted they had a better chance of survival if they stayed in their homes in Moab. Orpah stayed in Moab, but Ruth clung to Naomi with a commitment: "Your people shall be my people and your God, my God" (Ruth 1:16). Thus, we witness how the providence of God's intervention in Ruth's life would lead to His greater purpose of sending a Savior for all mankind. What an astounding miracle this is of witnessing how the tragic period of the time of the Judges takes a turn toward a future blessing being made possible through the life of Ruth, a pagan, Moabite woman. Consider how the providence of God was moving in the lives of Naomi and Ruth:

1. They returned to Bethlehem at the time of harvest, and through their situation would God again restore fullness to Naomi and Ruth (Ruth 1:19–22).
2. While working and gleaning in a certain field, Ruth discovered that it belonged to a wealthy man named Boaz, who happened to be a relative of Elimelech, Naomi's deceased husband. Was this by chance or God's providential hand? (Ruth 2:1–3).
3. Boaz, a wealthy, important man, would be able to act as Ruth's kinsman redeemer. This was not accidental but the work of God.
4. Boaz invited Ruth to work exclusively in his fields due to her good report and commitment to Naomi and even prayed that God would bless her (Ruth 2:4–18).
5. Naomi praised God when she realized that Boaz was a kinsman redeemer; she encouraged Ruth to follow his instructions (Ruth 2:20–3:6).
6. Naomi instructed Ruth to approach Boaz while he slept on the threshing floor. Ruth humbled herself and laid at his feet as one of his servants. She trusted God to use Boaz to answer her need. She made her request by

having him spread his garment since he was a kinsman redeemer. By this expression, Ruth was asking him for marriage. There was another qualified kinsman redeemer who could redeem Ruth, but he declined; thus, Boaz was free to marry Ruth (Ruth 3:7–4:12).

This touching story affirms how God's hand of providence, working behind the scenes in the lives of ordinary people, turns things toward His ultimate future plans. Again, this reaffirms that God is continually for us in every period of biblical history. This story serves as a transition from Judges to the future monarchy. Note that the book of Ruth ends by citing the genealogy that traces the lineage of Boaz from Perez, the son of Judah, down to King David (Ruth 4:18–22). Because of the faithfulness of Ruth and God's faithfulness, the genealogy points to the promise of the future Messiah through the line of David. Matthew 1:1 begins by stating, "The book of the genealogy of Jesus Christ the son of David, the son of Abraham ..."

Chapter 5

God's Providence through the Age of the Prophets

More attention is given to the earlier chapters since it was important to understand God's covenant plan being established by the patriarchs, Abraham, Isaac, and Jacob, and the importance of its being passed on to each future generation. As we now look at the historical activity of the prophets, let us consider a few introductory remarks to help us understand the purpose of the prophets. I don't want to get too technical here and confuse the purpose. It is important that you realize that the Bible is structured to reveal how God's purpose is developed.

The books of the law (Torah) represent the patriarchs, which include Abraham, Isaac, Jacob, Joseph, and Moses. They were under the covenant for establishing the nation of Israel. The prophets (Nebhim) represent former prophets: Joshua and the authors of Judges, 1 and 2 Samuel, and 1 and 2 Kings. These did not write but spoke prophetically even though they were not prophets as an institution. Joshua is included since he took the place of leadership after the death of Moses to take Israel into the land of Canaan.

The latter or major prophets (Nebhim)—Isaiah, Jeremiah, and Ezekiel—were writing prophets and formed the institution of prophets. The twelve minor prophets were those who operated as contemporaries with the major prophets—Hosea, Joel, Amos, Obadiah, Jonah, Micah Nahum, Habakkuk, Zephaniah, Haggai, and Malachi. Their prophecies were short written documents. The writings (Ketthubim) constituted the more devotional section of the canon, including Psalms, Job, and Proverbs. The books of the Megilloth (five scrolls) were designated for their feast days: Ruth was read at the Feast of Pentecost; Song of Songs was read at the Feast of Pentecost; Ecclesiastes at the Feast of Tabernacles; Esther at the Feast of Purim; and Lamentations was read concerning the destruction of Jerusalem. The books of Daniel, Ezra, Nehemiah, and 1&2 Chronicles represent historical books, tracing the journey of God's people.

HEBREW OLD TESTAMENT CANON

THE LAW (Torah)	THE PROPHETS (Nebhiim)	THE WRITINGS (Kethibhiim)
GENESIS	A. Former Prophets	PSALMS
EXODUS		JOB
LEVITICUS	JOSHUA	PROVERBS
NUMBERS	JUDGES (Non-literary	
DEUTERONOMY	I SAMUEL and	A. Megilloth
	II SAMUEL Non-institutional)	
[Pentateuch]	I KINGS	RUTH
	II KINGS	SONG OF SONGS
		ECCLESIASTES
	B. Latter Prophets	LAMENTATIONS
		ESTHER
	ISAIAH (Literary	
	JEREMIAH and	B. History
	EZEKIEL Institutional)	
	THE TWELVE	DANIEL
		EZRA/NEHEMIAH
		I CHRONICLES
		II CHRONICLES

Source: Modern Jewish arrangement in modern Jewish editions of the Old Testament. Geisler and Nix, 1979.

It is interesting that in **Luke 11:49–51,** Jesus, in referring to the scriptures while talking to the Pharisees, affirms the beginning and end of the canon of scripture.

"Therefore the wisdom of God also said, I will send them prophets and apostles, and some of them they will kill and persecute, that the blood responsible for the blood of all the prophets which was shed from the foundation of the world may be required of this generation. From the blood of Abel (Genesis) to the blood of Zechariah who perished between the altar and the temple (Chronicles)".

Jesus was referring to the whole canon of scripture that I have referred to above. I remember when I was first exposed to the canon of scripture during my training as a minister—I felt it had no relevance to my future work. However, when I realized how it made Bible history so meaningful to God's redemptive purpose for the world He created, the Bible became alive and challenging. I trust that as you follow my purpose in this course, you will appreciate how God is for us in every situation of Bible history. I need to confess that I never appreciated history. It seemed boring and meaningless to me. But when I discovered how biblical history revealed the very heart and character of God for humanity and His constant intervention to direct them to His eternal purpose, I developed a whole different attitude toward all the biblical events. I would like to encourage you, the readers, to continue to discern how God has worked and is working for us and preparing us for our future life in eternity. I believe that when we get to heaven, we will be overwhelmed to realize that God has worked since the beginning of time for our eternal joy and happiness.

Chapter 6

God's Love for Us Extended to the Monarchy Period

The books of 1 and 2 Samuel introduced us to a serious transition in the life of Israel. They desired to be governed by a king much like other surrounding nations. The Edomites, Moabites, and Ammonites all had kings who were absolute in their power. They were tired of the rule of the judges, who caused them to become frequently divided and oppressed. Before the period of the judges, they were constituted as a theocracy (God's rule). Their cry for a king was somewhat acceptable to God if they would choose a king who would walk in the ways of the Lord. But unfortunately, in their request for a king like other nations, it was more than likely that they would adopt their gods and rituals. Samuel warned them of such dangers, and he reminded them that they were not rejecting him but actually rejecting God (1 Sam. 8:6–7). Samuel further warned them what it meant to adopt the behavior of the king they would adopt to reign over them (**1 Sam. 8:10–18).** However, the people refused to obey Samuel's admonition. God told Samuel to heed their voice and make them a king **(1 Sam. 8:19–22).** Samuel now became God's last judge and first prophet. An interesting observation is found in the following:

> **"1&2 Samuel reflect accurately both the necessity of kingship and the dangerous implications of**

such a move. **God's use of kingship as part of the preparation for the King of Kings is witness to the validity monarchy in Israel.... The truly successful pattern of government for Israel was a delicate balance—not theocracy or monarchy but theocracy through monarchy. God must always be the true ruler if Israel was to be his people."** (LaSor and Eerdmans 1982, 34)

God's ultimate purpose is to keep His covenant with his current people as well as future generations. In some respects a monarchy was a serious turning point, but it was necessary for Israel's survival. They needed strong leadership to unite them in their present condition under the judges. They were rejecting theocracy for monarchy, but actually God must be their true ruler. A possible balance could be a theocracy though monarchy. God could exercise His rule through a human king, but it would always result in great tension. The people's choice of Saul was a terrible mistake and created havoc for Israel. God accepted their choice, but David would be His divine choice. I believe God allowed the reign of Saul so that Israel would realize it had been a poor choice and God's choice of David was best.

The Death of Saul and the Rise of David as King (1 Samuel 31–2 Samuel 2:1–7)

Saul was critically wounded in the battle against the Philistines. It is possible that his fear of being mutilated and tortured led him to ask his armor-bearer to run him through with his sword, but the armor-bearer refused. So Saul took his own sword and fell upon it, killing himself (1 Sam. 31:4–5). Saul's reign ended in complete failure due to his lack of godliness. He was a pathetic example of carnal willfulness. Even the best of his abilities finally failed him when God forsook him. It appears that his death was a stroke of divine judgment: "So Saul died for his transgression which he committed against the Lord ... and also asking counsel of one that had a familiar spirit, to enquire of it. So the LORD put him to death and turned the kingdom over to David's son Jesse" (1 Chron. 10:13–14). Here again we witness the hand of God in this situation.

The book of 2 Samuel deals almost exclusively with the history of David—not with the whole of it, for it begins in 1 Samuel and continues into 1 Kings. The people clamored for a king, and God gave them one after their own heart (Saul); He then gave them one after His own heart (David).

David Anointed King Over Judah (2 Samuel 2–4)

David's reign over Judah was seven and one half years with Hebron as the capital, reigning only over his own tribe. However, Abner, who was captain of Saul's armies, proceeded to select and name as king Ishbosheth, fourth son of Saul, who proceeded to rule as king of the entire nation. But in reality, he was a weak ruler who was dominated by Abner. As the years passed, the house of David became increasingly strong, while the house of Saul continued to weaken. Interestingly, the relationship between Abner and Ishbosheth caused Abner to resign his support, and lo and behold Abner began supporting David and convinced him of his sincerity. When Joab, who led the forces for David, heard about this, he was furious because Abner was responsible for the death of his brother Asahel. So he tricked Abner into exposing his true self and murdered him (2 Sam. 3:6–27). Chapter 4 records the death of Ishbosheth by two of his own captains.

David in the Process of Time Becomes King Over All Israel (2 Samuel 5)

Now, once again, we see an opportunity for the hand of God to intervene and redirect the situation to His purposes.

Remember, everything that takes place throughout Bible history is directed toward humankind's future welfare. We are now entering a more organized situation involving monarchy (single rule), which exemplifies the ultimate rule of God in all things. It is not my intent to rehearse the whole history of this period of David and Solomon's kingdom rule. But one of the key factors in this period of history is that we have reached an important summit of the Old Testament—God's promise to David of an everlasting kingdom. The covenant with David is in the background of every page of the rest of the Bible—indeed into the last page of the book of Revelation. Revelation 22:16 says, "I, Jesus, have sent My angel to testify to you these things in the churches. I am the Root (origin) and offspring (descendant) of David." The story of the Bible is a history of salvation—God's desire and plan to bestow His blessing, the gift of His divine life, on all creation. What is God's purpose with His covenant? To bless the human race, transforming it into a single family of God, to make each individual what Adam was intended to be—a son of God the most high, heir of the kingdom of heaven. These are days of immense significance to the church and the believers in Jesus Christ. The Lord Jesus Christ is coming back soon to take His people home and thereafter to establish His kingdom.

David's Grievous Mistake and Its Tragic Results (2 Samuel 11 and 12)

In spite of David's experience with God, who declared that he was a man after His own heart (Acts 13:22), David's sin with Bathsheba is a lesson in the power of temptation. David Jeremiah observes that David went wrong for several reasons.

1. He ignored his place (2 Sam. 11:1); he remained in Jerusalem while his troops went to battle.

2. He indulged in his passion (2 Sam. 11:2); he initiated the proposition (2 Sam. 11:3).
3. He ignored the prohibition (2 Sam. 11:3) in *Teaching Points of Anatomy of a Temptation* (Jeremiah Bible, 414).

God did not break His covenant made to David because it was not a conditional covenant. However, God was not pleased with David's sins of adultery and murder. God sent the prophet Nathan, who presented a parable, a subtle yet forceful rebuke of David (2 Sam. 12:1–14). The king, whose chief obligation was to enforce the terms of covenants and ensure justice at every level of society, had grossly violated the covenant himself. God's mercy was his only hope. Although his sin had dire effects such as the death of Bathsheba's baby (2 Sam. 12:15–19), mercy spared him. David's powerful prayers of repentance recorded in Psalms 32 and 51 reveal that no sin is beyond Almighty God to forgive. This is more evidence that God is for us at all times and in all situations if we come to Him in confession and repentance when necessary.

In his last hours David prayed to God that He would give his son Solomon a loyal heart to keep God's commandments and statutes. Now Solomon was anointed king. Solomon sat on the throne of the Lord as king instead of David and prospered, and all Israel obeyed him (1 Chron. 20:23–25).

What Are the Highlights of Solomon's Life?

When he ascended to the throne, Solomon sought God, and God gave him the opportunity to ask whatever he wanted. Solomon humbly acknowledged his inability to rule well and asked God for wisdom to rule God's people justly. God gave him both wisdom and wealth (1 Kings 3:4; 10:37). In fact, his riches and wisdom surpassed those of all the kings of the earth (1 Kings 1:23). God also gave him peace on all sides during his reign (1 Kings 4:20–25). He completed many building projects, especially the great temple of God. He also built a fleet of ships and acquired tons of gold from Ophir with Hiram, king of Tyre, as a partner. Later he acquired seven hundred wives and three hundred concubines. Many of them were foreigners who led him into public idolatry in his old age, greatly angering God (1 Kings 11:1–13). It's sad that some people start out well but later fail. Before God's patience with the waywardness of Solomon finally wore out, He sent His sentence of judgment to the king, probably through a prophet, much like He sent the prophet Nathan to David. This did not cause God to cancel His promise to David through the tribe of Judah and ultimately through the Messiah. In spite of all these things, the desire of God to bless and protect people throughout the ages still stands!

The Legacies of Both David and Solomon Reveal How God Is for Us

David wrote many psalms (seventy-five) which, in a sense, were devotionals. One of the most revealing about his life is the Shepherd's Psalm, Psalm 23. The history of David often has a tendency to focus on his weaknesses and blinds us to his heart's true strength. The psalms constitute the devotional aspects of the Hebrew people in contrast to the law and the prophets. Psalm 23 gives us a picture of complete peacefulness and rest in trusting God. Read this psalm and get the sense of God being for us:

The Lord is my shepherd; I shall not want. He makes me to lie down in green pastures; He leads me beside the still waters. He restores my soul; He leads me in the paths of righteousness for His name's sake. Yea, though I walk through the valley of the shadow of death, I will fear no evil; for you are with me. You prepare a table for me in the presence of my enemies;

> you anoint my head with oil; my cup runs over.
> Surely goodness and mercy shall follow me all
> the days of my life and I will dwell in the house
> of the LORD forever.

Solomon contributed his wisdom that he received from God
in the books of Proverbs, Ecclesiastes, and Song of Solomon.

- **Proverbs:** When Solomon succeeded his father, David, as king, it certainly required great responsibility and wisdom. When God appeared to Solomon and said to him, "Ask! What shall I give you?" Solomon answered, "Give me wisdom and knowledge that I may go out and come in before this people, for who can judge this great people of Yours?" **(1 Chron. 1:10)**. God granted his request. Solomon wrote a number of proverbs that we may know wisdom and instruction. They provided practical wisdom for everyday life.
- **Ecclesiastes:** Solomon poses the question, "Is there anything new under the sun?" The answer he gives is, "Meaningless, meaningless, says the teacher, utterly meaningless. Everything is meaningless! What does a man gain from all his labor at which he toils under the sun?" (Ecc. 1: 3, 9) The basic point Solomon is trying to express is that if there is nothing above the sun, then life is meaningless! However, if there is meaning above the sun (God), then all is not vanity. This again expresses that God is for us and life is worth-living.
- **Song of Solomon:** This book is a practical love story. "There is no love song that compares with that of Solomon and his Lebanese Shulamite farmgirl turned queen" (David Jeremiah's introduction in his study Bible, p. 865). It is a human and holy love story inspired by a holy God. God is very interested in marital love that

involves His idea and approval. Is there any doubt that God is for us in all stages of our life?

The Presence and Activity of God during the Death of My First Wife

I actively experienced the love of God through many of my Christian friends from various churches and teaching colleagues when my wife was ill. A local nursing village provided care for her during my college teaching responsibility at no charge. I will be eternally grateful to those who came alongside during this time. Eventually, God took her home. As I went to the hospital, I was approached by two nurses who wanted to go with me to her room. They were Christians and wanted to pray with me. They informed me that she had died peacefully. However, the amazing thing was that the hospital had no record of these nurses. They simply disappeared, and I believe they were ministering spirits from God!

Chapter 7

The Tragic Division of the Kingdom to Captivity

King Solomon's achievements and failures are documented in 1 Kings 3–11. Some of his achievements are as follows:

1. He built a temple for God in Jerusalem as a fulfillment of God's promises to David.
2. He collected and composed thousands of proverbs and songs that have been used in teaching and worship.
3. He established and developed trade links with other countries, which led to economic prosperity in Israel. He was a successful merchant.
4. Solomon initiated industrial activities and exploited copper deposits in the area of Edom, which had been conquered by David.
5. He developed diplomatic relations with foreign countries by marrying the daughters of the kings of those countries.
6. Solomon brought the ark of the covenant to the temple of Jerusalem, which represented God's presence among His people (1 Kings 8).

However, Solomon's life also included many failures. He took his eyes and heart off of God and embraced idolatry and immorality. We need to realize that when we truly make God the focus and meaning of our lives, we can always be assured that

God is for us. You cannot play with sin's fire and not get burned. No matter how much a person like Solomon has accomplished and contributed to God's work in the world, vices can overcome virtues. He not only pursued many foreign wives but also their gods. We need to take heed that our idols and vices could seduce us and, like Solomon, turn our hearts from God. His downfall was hastened by the building of shrines for the gods of his foreign wives and resulted in his turning away from the worship of Jehovah.

He also imposed heavy taxation on his subjects and districts in order to raise part of the government revenue. He killed his half-brother Adonjah (1 Kings 2) because he suspected that Adonjah could be his rival.

The Divided Monarchy (1 Kings 12:1–2 Kings 18:12)

This time in biblical history was a tragic time for God's ancient people. I will not attempt to unravel it completely because of its many facets. It would appear that God had abandoned His people and their future, but it was not so. God was still for them and would deal with them. My intent is to carry you briefly through this time and deal enough with the highlights in order for you to see God's hand again in this time.

The Divided Period as Found in 1 Kings 11–20 and 2 Kings

Solomon's death brought a new king to the throne, Solomon's son Rehoboam. This transition brought to the surface all the latent feelings of oppression and abuse that had been suppressed under the rule of David and Solomon. A civil war broke out as Solomon's sons and generals fought for the throne. Rehoboam had his father's blessing to be the new king, but his brother Jeroboam had more military influence. In the end, Rehoboam took the southern half of the country and called it Judah, while Jeroboam took the northern half and kept the name Israel. Each claimed to be God's chosen king. Despite the warnings from many prophets, both kingdoms repeatedly turned from God. Assyria and Babylon forced the divided kingdoms into exile. Jerusalem and the temple were destroyed. The tribe of Judah endured seventy years of exile and then returned to rebuild with the guidance of Zerubbabel, Ezra, and Nehemiah. God was with them through it all, helping His people to triumph. The Babylonian exile of the southern kingdom occurred over the course of three major deportations. Among the captives were Daniel and Ezekiel. While they were exiled at slightly different times, both of their ministries bear witness to the fact that God did not abandon his people in the darkest times. Rather, God held out to the exiles the pledge that his salvation would come, slowly but surely. While Daniel and Ezekiel spoke from Babylon, Jeremiah was among the remnant left in the now desolate promised land. These three prophets give us a window into the lives of those in the kingdom of Judah who experienced the darkness of the Babylonian exile and waited in hope. I trust you are beginning to understand and see that God is with His people through every difficult situation. It is important to understand that your security is not found in the world's system but rather in God's kingdom through Jesus Christ and His salvation offered to you.

The Post-Exilic Period: Rebuilding the Walls of Jerusalem and the Temple with Nehemiah and Ezra

Ezra and Nehemiah are one unified book in the Hebrew Bible. They tell one story in twenty-three chapters: rebuilding the temple (Ezra) and the walls (Nehemiah) of Jerusalem. The book of Ezra is clearly divisible into two parts that cover the first and second returns of the exiles from Persia to Jerusalem.

Rebuilding the Temple (Ezra 1:1–6:22)

The Lord inspired Cyrus to permit the return of the Jews to worship their God. The foundation of the temple was laid, and people worshiped God. But opposition from their enemies stopped the work. The Lord stirred up the people through the prophets Zechariah and Haggai to complete the work in spite of the resistance. King Darius authorized and funded the project, which was completed with great celebration. However, the walls needed to be restored for the protection of the temple. Thus, the work of Nehemiah became very vital.

Nehemiah continues the story of the restored community, whereas the book of Ezra focuses on the religious restoration of Jerusalem. The fact that God has not given up on His people is exemplified at this time. The book of Nehemiah is particularly concerned with the account of the erection of the walls of Jerusalem. The Jews had been in their land for almost a century, but they had made no attempt to rebuild until Nehemiah came on the scene. Nehemiah was a cupbearer to King Artaxerxes of Persia, which gave him personal contact with the monarch, Nehemiah's brother Hanani. He reported the condition of Jerusalem as being in ruins, not only because of the seventh-century Babylonian siege but also because of recent attacks by the Samaritans. Nehemiah's reaction to the news was to weep and mourn, and he was moved to fasting and prayer. His prayer was that God would vindicate Himself and His promises and grant to Nehemiah the ability to restore the Jerusalem wall. Nehemiah was given a royal commission to undertake the rebuilding of Jerusalem, as well as provisions necessary to do the job (Neh. 1–2). The opponents of Nehemiah were the Samaritan leaders, Sanballet, Tobiah, and Geshem, who was probably the governor of Samaria. These men, both by physical opposition and moral intimidation, sought to hinder Nehemiah's agenda.

When Nehemiah heard that Jerusalem was unprotected, he sought God's help through fasting and prayer. His appeal was based on God's covenant with Israel as given in Deuteronomy. There the Lord threatened the unfaithful but also promised to assist the repentant (see Deut. 9:29; 28:14; 30:1–4). In summary, the gates and walls were restored (3:1–32) and prayer for God's intervention to the opposition was answered. (4:1–23). Completion of the wall occurred in spite of opposition (Ch. 6). There was revival under Ezra and Nehemiah. Ezra ministered the book of the law of Moses to the people, and they were joyfully receptive to the Word; on the following day, they observed the Feast of the Tabernacles and promptly set about to achieve the wall's restoration. The enthusiasm of the people in observing the divine ordinances is impressive testimony to the effectiveness of the Word of God in fostering revival. Once again, the restoration of the temple and the rebuilding of the wall is another historical testimony that God is with His people to help them to continue to trust Him and serve Him. Unfortunately, the survival of the Jews as a people committed to God demanded exclusion of the Gentiles for a time. However, the future history includes the Gentiles, and the survival of the church demands inclusion of all who will hear the gospel and commit their lives to Christ.

My Challenge to Restore Local Brethren in Christ

While I was actively engaged in my college teaching ministry, I was approached to help a local church in Dillsburg, Pennsylvania, that was struggling to keep operating without a permanent pastor. Since I previously had a number of years of pastoral ministry and especially church planting experiencing, I was approached regarding my availability. The dean of the college was very sympathetic toward this church's situation and was willing to reduce my teaching load to half time if the church would subsidize my teaching salary. The proposal was accepted by the church, and I began my pastoral ministry with the hope of stimulating growth. To my amazement, the congregation began to grow in significant numbers as many of the college students began to attend. The church had little foyer space, so the students stayed outside until the doors were opened. The people of the neighborhood were surprised to see all these students gathered for church. The church began to grow and prosper, and people began joining our worship to the point that many students sat in the church aisles to accommodate the adults attending. God truly blessed the ministry, which eventually led to our considering additional space. After two years the church had prospered to the point that the college asked me to decide whether I wanted to work full-time teaching or pastoring. I knew that God had called me to be a teacher, so the church was able to hire a new pastor and I returned to my college teaching. The church had grown to approximately three hundred and is still functioning today. It was the closest thing to a revival I'd ever experienced. We should always be ready and willing to step into new situations where God wants to use us. We must always be discerning that God is actively moving in our lives, pulling us from our comfort zone to accomplish His will and eternal purpose. *God is for us in restoring situations as He has been throughout history.*

Chapter 8

A Brief Focus on Two Major Prophets: Isaiah and Malachi

Isaiah portrays the coming Messiah in two ways: as the "Suffering Servant" who bears the sins of His people (Isa. 53:1–12) and as the glorified King and counselor whose rule over His people will have no end (Isa. 9:6–7; 11:1–10). By the time of Christ, Isaiah establishes that God's purpose was to make salvation available through the Jews to the Gentiles (Isa. 24:15; 42:4, 6, 10, 12; 49:1, 6; 60:3, 9; *Jeremiah Bible*, p. 88). This is additional proof that God is for us by Isaiah's proclamation of the future coming of Christ and His purpose to bring salvation to us.

The book of Isaiah has been called the Fifth Gospel, and Isaiah has also been called the Fifth Evangelist. Christ's virgin birth, His character, His life, His death, His resurrection, and His second coming are all presented in Isaiah with clearness and definiteness.

Malachi is the last prophetic message from God before the close of the Old Testament period and provides a transition for understanding the kingdom proclamation in Malachi 3:1:

> "Behold, I send My messenger, and he will prepare the way before Me. And the Lord, whom you seek, will suddenly come into His temple, even the Messenger of the covenant, in whom you delight. Behold, He is coming," says the Lord of hosts.

We have traveled briefly through a large portion of the Old Testament in order that we may see the extent to which God has gone to reveal Himself through His covenant. As we move into the New Testament, we will see how God made the ultimate revelation of Himself in His Son, Jesus Christ, through whom salvation was offered to all humankind. Here we have the closing of the Old Testament and the promise of great things to come. The messenger of the covenant is none other than John the Baptist, who will introduce Jesus as the promised Messiah (Jesus) who will make salvation possible for those who will accept Him and as a result prove that God is definitely for us now and in our future.

Part 2

Evidence That God Is for Us in the New Testament

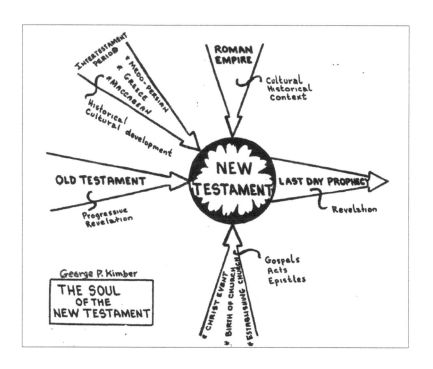

INTERTESTAMENT PERIOD
* MEDO-PERSIAN
* GREECE
* MACCABEAN

Historical Cultural development

ROMAN EMPIRE

Cultural Historical Context

OLD TESTAMENT

NEW TESTAMENT

LAST DAY PROPHECY

Revelation

Progressive Revelation

George P. Kimber

THE SOUL OF THE NEW TESTAMENT

* CHRIST EVENT
* BIRTH OF CHURCH
* ESTABLISHING CHURCH

Gospels
Acts
Epistles

Chapter 9

The New Testament Revelation That God Is for Us Was the Jesus Advent

The Old Testament people of Israel were constantly in expectation of the coming of their Messiah. Their hope had been shattered until it appeared that God's promised Messiah would be announced by His messenger John the Baptist, the messenger of their covenant. However, in many ways they misunderstood God's covenant with them. They did not have discernment of the last message of the prophet Malachi. Their years of anticipating the coming of the Messiah had now become confusing because they could not comprehend that Jesus was the fulfillment of the messianic promise. Now God is fully revealing that He is for us through the life and ministry of Jesus Christ, God in the flesh!

The early Christians did not believe that the time and place of the birth of Jesus was left to chance. On the contrary, as we have been moving through the Old Testament, we have witnessed, as they did, the hand of God preparing the advent of Jesus in all the events prior to the birth and all the historical circumstances around it. The New Testament continues in a larger and more precise way of expressing how God is for us. God was moving through His actions in the Old Testament to His larger revelation to us. The scriptures declare in Galatians 4:4, "But *when the time had fully come,* God sent forth His Son, born of woman, born under the law" (emphasis added).

The coming of Jesus Christ to Palestine, fulfilling the many messianic prophecies, is the introduction of God's invading His world from this part of the globe. I want to stress, as I have earlier, that God's entrance into the time dimension was to begin to fulfill His purposes, most importantly to reveal again that He created time as a parentheses between eternity past and eternity future. This is when He will usher in all the redeemed to their heavenly home. I have adopted this concept to teach and encourage people to take advantage of this truth because it definitely reveals that God is for us now and in the future. We need to take advantage of the time we have to accept His plan for our eternal destiny. I believe we are experiencing that in this very hour. Time as we know it seems to be moving in fast-forward as the result of our technological advances and commitment to His will for us. Let us give attention to the Word of God as it displays God's hand in the New Testament and the developing historical events toward the end time. We, as never before, need to be discerning of how God has been continually moving in New Testament times and toward the future and the second coming of Jesus in the near future. It is important that we trust the Word of God and be ready to meet Him at that time.

The Importance of Christ's Coming in This World as a Baby

In order for us to understand that Jesus Christ is for us, He deliberately came personally through the human birth process. Why? So He could experience our humanity and help us understand how much God is for us! The prophecy of Isaiah 7:14 is fulfilled in Christ's birth. He was called Immanuel, which means "God with us." He was born with both human and divine natures. Just think! The Godhead has ordained to be actually visible through Jesus Christ, the Son of God. Certainly we can take heart in the fact that God is serious and concerned for His creation, especially the human beings He created to inhabit this world and hopefully the perfect world to come in eternity, the purpose of God the Father, Jesus Christ, and Holy Spirit in history. Let us again be reminded of the message of John 3:16–17:

> For God so loved the world that He gave His only begotten Son, that whoever believes in Him should not perish but have everlasting life. For God sent not His Son into the world to condemn the world, but that the world through Him might be saved.

These two verses tell us more about God and His plan for us than any other verses in the entire Bible. Can there be any doubt that God is for us with such love and passion that He would eventually allow His Son to be humiliated, scorned, and crucified on a cross for you and me and the whole world? But also realize that Jesus was submitting to the Father's will in all of this, for you and me and the world, that would satisfy His holiness and be able to grant us salvation and eternal life. Thank God that Jesus was able to be resurrected from the grave and now sits at the right hand of His Father, making intercession for us that we may have the opportunity to receive eternal life! The Holy Spirit was sent to initiate the work of redemption and regeneration by literally entering our lives and making Christ real and personable. The Holy Spirit brings honor to the Father and glorifies the Son. We are thus "born again" by the Spirit and ordained to be part of the eternal kingdom. Regeneration by the Holy Spirit brings new life in Christ. I trust you are beginning to understand that God is working in us and for us. The four gospels were written by the early disciples, who thought it necessary that the life of Jesus Christ be presented to attract the attention, win the allegiance, and strengthen the faith of each person and therefore reveal that God is for all people.

Matthew, the publican, a Jew, and one of the twelve, wrote to convince the Jews that although they had crucified Jesus because they did not believe He was their Messiah, He was the fulfillment of the prophecy of the promised Messiah. He traced the lineage of Jesus from Abraham through David to prove that Jesus was the heir to the throne and thereby the King of the Jews.

Mark, Peter's amanuensis (a person who writes from dictation), wrote to the Romans that Jesus was a man of power in every way and worthy of their attention, respect, reverence, and worship. In spite of their earlier actions against Jesus, He was for them as their Savior if they believed.

Luke, a companion of Paul, a Greek historian, and a physician but not one of the twelve, wrote to convince the Greeks that this Jesus was one with whom companionship might be enjoyed and one who might satisfy their longings. He wrote that Jesus was a sympathetic savior, a perfect "Son of Man," and traced His lineage back to Adam, thus identifying his humanity.

John, the beloved disciple, wrote to convince all Christians that they may believe that Jesus is the Christ and, by believing, may have life through His name. He taught that Jesus is the glorious, only begotten Son and God manifest in the flesh, the Son of God—again, for all to understand that God is for all who believe.

Chapter 10

The Ministry of Jesus Christ

The entire ministry of Jesus Christ was devoted to revealing the love of God for all humanity. John the Baptist was ordained by God to be the forerunner declaring the person of Christ. The prophet Malachi had identified a preparatory messenger like Elijah four hundred years earlier. Jesus later identified the messenger as John the Baptist, who came in the spirit and power of Elijah (Matt. 11:1–14). Let us consider some of Jesus's ministries during His time on earth that reveal His love and desire for us to know that God is for us.

Significant Miracles of Jesus That Reveal His Love and Care for Humanity

- *The Wedding at Cana of Galilee (John 2:1–12):* We understand that the hospitality shown by people of the East was always a sacred duty. At a wedding Jesus was attending, they had run out of wine, which would have brought embarrassment, shame, and humiliation. His mother, Mary, instinctively turned to Jesus whenever anything went wrong. She knew her son. Jesus responded, "My hour has not yet come." Nevertheless, Mary instructed the servants to do what Jesus would tell them to do. Jesus revealed that His ultimate mission was to reveal God's desire for us to know that He cares for us and will help in times of trouble. He instructed the servants to retrieve wine from vases that contained water, which Jesus miraculously changed into just enough wine to solve the problem.

- *Healing of a Leper (Luke 5:12–16):* Jesus's disciples traveled with Him and learned from Him. In one of the towns they visited, a man with leprosy was suffering not only from physical agony but also from the stigma of being shunned by the community. In his desperation he fell face down at the feet of Jesus and begged for help, saying, "Lord, if you are willing, you can make me clean." He believed Jesus could heal him. Jesus said, "I am willing; be made clean," and immediately the disease left him. Does Jesus care? Certainly! He still cares for us today.

- *Calming the Storm (Mark 4:35–41):* It was Jesus's idea to cross over to the other side of the body of water. A great storm arose, and the waves were filling the boat. Jesus was in the stern asleep on a pillow. The disciples were professional fishermen, yet they were afraid for their lives! In their panic they cried out, "Do you not care that we are perishing?" Jesus certainly cared; he stood up and commanded the sea and wind to cease. He then confronted them concerning their lack of faith. They suddenly became fearful and aware that Jesus was demonstrating His power as God. He revealed that He cared for them at this time. It is interesting that Jesus, in rebuking the wind and the waves, said "Peace be still," which in the Greek text literally means be "muzzled." When they continued toward shore, they were going to be confronted by a demon-possessed man whom Jesus would rebuke and heal, or "muzzle." Jesus was revealing His power and caring toward this man using the same power He had used to still the storm. Does Jesus care? Yes, in many ways.

- *Feeding of the Five Thousand (Matt. 14:13–21):* Let us consider one more incident proving that God cares for us. The miracle of the feeding of the five thousand demonstrates how Jesus cared about those people who were there without food. He requested that a boy who had small amount of bread give it to Him, and He miraculously multiplied and had it distributed among the five thousand—with some left over. Jesus cares enough to do whatever is required, even a miracle. Let me repeat the most central scripture within the New Testament:

> For God so loved the world that He gave His only begotten Son, that whoever believes in Him should not perish but have everlasting life. For God did not send His Son into the world to condemn the world but that the world through Him might be saved. (John 3:16–17)

I remember some years ago during the so-called Jesus Movement that took place across the country when many young people were evangelizing and witnessing the gospel. It was an attempt to move outside the institutional church into the streets and witness to individuals everywhere. Many lives were touched but not without some difficult situations. A number of incidents occurred where people questioned whether Jesus cared about them in light of what seemed to be confusing messages being expressed throughout many different denominations.

I remember one particular incident where a black girl was approached by one of the witnesses. He asked her, "Did you know that Jesus loves you and wants to come into your heart?" She replied, "No! Only if he would appear in black skin!" This girl was expressing that as far as she knew, Jesus only appeared to love "white folk." She was expressing her dilemma: "Does He care about black people?" She went on to say, "You wouldn't understand unless you were in black skin. You love me as I am and then, maybe, I would understand that God is for me and loves me."

This may appear to be a harsh indictment against the church and our witness, but it certainly should make us stop and think of how we represent God's love and message that He desires people to know and accept His caring heart. We need to be more aware that we are expressing the heart and love of Jesus and the Word of God and not our own opinion or the culture. Remember, God loves the whole world in spite of all the divisions we make concerning people and their worth. I often think of our missionaries, many of whom leave the comfort of their own homes and lives to bring God's message to those who have never heard it or who are in bondage in their countries ruled by dictators or leaders who keep them from hearing the Word of God and His love for them. Once they are exposed to the Word of God, they have the privilege of knowing that the God of the Bible is a God who is for them. One of the growing concerns in the many missionary endeavors is training people within their cultures to preach and teach their own people, which would be more effective and lasting. One of the most successful operations in this effort is the Wycliffe Global Alliance, which develops the scriptures within the languages of the people. Their goal is to accomplish this in as many countries as possible.

Chapter 11

The Death and Resurrection
of Jesus Christ

One of the most controversial yet most important incidents in the scriptures is the death and resurrection of Jesus Christ. There are still a number of teachers and scholars who are skeptical of these events. On the other hand, these events express the ultimate desire on the part of God the Father to make possible our salvation and eternal destiny.

What Does the Cross Mean to Us?

In keeping with my purpose for writing this book, which is revealing evidence that God is for us, I certainly need to disclose how the death and resurrection demonstrate God's love and concern for us. In order for God to accomplish His will for us, it was necessary to have a sacrifice to appease His holiness and position. He could not entertain or approach sin without judging it. There would have to be a sufficient sacrifice that would appease His holiness. His only Son offered Himself as that offering. Through human thinking, we could not comprehend this process. It was the only way He could accomplish His purpose to redeem humankind and grant them eternal life in His heavenly kingdom. In order to really understand how much He is for us and our future, let us briefly consider what it meant for Jesus to die on the earthly cross to accomplish His Father's wishes.

- *Substitution:* Christ died for *our sins*, the righteous for the unrighteous, to bring us to God (1 Peter 1:18). The apostle John states in his epistle, "He laid down His life for us" (1 John 1:16). The Bible tells us that death is the result of sin, so Jesus, being sinless, was bearing sin's penalty (which he did not deserve) in place of others, you and me. This was the most amazing act of love ever known.
- *Propitiation:* This means appeasing an offended person by paying the penalty he or she demands for the offense. This enables one to receive back into his or her favor the person who committed the offense. This is where we get the idea of atonement, which means that the offender and the person offended can be "at one."
- *Redemption:* When the redemption is paid, the captives are set free; this is what happens for those to whom Jesus gave his life (see Gal. 3:13). The ransom price of Jesus's death satisfied God's justice.
- Forgiveness of Sins (Eph. 1:7) and Reconciliation (Rom. 5:10): These are also the result of the sacrifice of Jesus and give us justification (Rom. 5:1). This is the position before God as "not guilty" because His death paid in full the penalty that God's law demands. To be justified means to be right with God for time and eternity.

The Proof of Promises Fulfilled: Christ's Resurrection

After Jesus died and was buried, He rose from the dead. In certain circles of Christianity, the cross is displayed with Jesus's body hanging on it. Certainly we need to be reminded of this, but it completely misrepresents the Christian message. The symbol of Christianity is an empty cross because the Bible's wonderful message is that Jesus Christ is alive today and is at the right hand of the Father. Furthermore, one day we will stand before this throne in awe of what God has done for us. The Holy Spirit and the scriptures allow us to know and sense this truth!

Think about all this. Why would anyone doubt that God loves us and is for us? God has been at work from the beginning of Adam and Eve's sin that diverted God's original plan for populating heaven. The angels continue to serve God's desire and are ministering spirits to fulfill God's eternal plan. We will experience a wonderful revelation of the glorious realm of heaven and eternal happiness that will surpass any happiness we have experienced on earth. The eye has not seen neither has it entered the heart for the glory that God has prepared for the redeemed.

Chapter 12

The Holy Spirit at Pentecost
and the Birth of the Church:
The Apostolic Age (AD 30–100)

We have been beholding the wonder of Jesus Christ and His redemptive work directed toward our future. We now come to the most outstanding events following the resurrection of Christ—the sending of the Holy Spirit upon believers and the birth of the church. These events reveal in a positive way that God is determined to have a people, His church, to spread the news that God is for us and wants to use us for His glory.

The Role of the Holy Spirit Assisting the Work of the Father and the Son

We need to understand that there is only one God, eternally existing and fully expressed in three entities: the Father, the Son, and the Holy Spirit. Each member of the Godhead is equally God—not three gods but three entities of one Godhead. Even though this is difficult for us to fully comprehend, we must still trust the scriptures' declaration. The Holy Spirit is fully God. He eternally exists along with the Father and the Son. The following diagram might help you understand the divine Godhead.

THE DIVINE GODHEAD

	Function		Purpose
	FATHER	Decrees the Plan	
ONE ESSENCE	THE SON	Provides the Means	REDEMPTION
	HOLY SPIRIT	Executes the Plan	

The scriptures clearly reveal the Trinity, even though our rational minds cannot fully comprehend God functioning in three persons but one essence to accomplish an eternal purpose. Consider how God is working for your eternal destiny. God is for us! When we accept Jesus Christ as our Savior, the Holy Spirit indwells our souls, and we experience salvation evidenced by the Spirit's indwelling. Listen to the message of the Gospel of John and consider the incident with Nicodemus, a ruler of the Jews (John 3). Nicodemus, a man of the Pharisees, was fascinated by the miracles of Jesus and came to Him by night so that his fellow Pharisees would not know he had gone. He refers to Jesus as Rabbi because rabbis were known to have long discussions with their disciples at times. Nicodemus greeted Jesus as a teacher who came from God. He did not recognize that Jesus was God Himself rather than a representative of God. However, he seemed to sense there was something different about Jesus as he expressed, "No one can do these signs that you do unless God is with him" (John 3:2). Jesus, in effect, said to him that one cannot see or understand who He is unless one is born again spiritually. Nicodemus became confused and inquired, "How can one be born a second time? (John 3:4). Jesus's answer indicates how this is possible: "I tell you the truth, no one can enter the kingdom of God unless he is born of water and the Spirit. Flesh gives birth to flesh, but the Spirit gives birth to spirit." (John 3:5). The important thing I am emphasizing is that in order for you to really understand and know God, you must know His Son, Jesus, as savior through the indwelling of the Holy Spirit. That gives you spiritual birth! Here again, we understand how much God is for us!

The Miracle of Pentecost and the Birth of the Church

The church is a new work of God begun in the New Testament. I am sure that many of you recognize what constitutes the church in terms of buildings and cathedrals and multiple denominations. This has resulted in so much confusion because it raises the question, Which church is the one that God has ordained? In turn, this brings confusion and speculation to our society. First, let us discover the origin of the church that God has ordained and its overall purpose.

In Matthew 16:13–20, Jesus asked His disciples, "Who do men say that I, the Son of man, am?" They said, "Some John the Baptist, some Elijah, and others Jeremiah or one of the prophets." Then Jesus asked, "But who do you say I am?" (Matt. 16:13–14). At that point Simon Peter spoke up and said, "You are the Christ, the Son of the living God." (Matt. 16:16). Jesus responded that Peter hadn't come to this conclusion by himself but that this was a revelation given to Peter from the Father above (Matt. 16:17). Jesus then said to Peter, "You are Peter (Petros, a small rock), but I am going to build My Church on the rock (Petra, a large massive rock) of your confession of which the very gates of Hell cannot prevail" (Matt. 16:18–19). Jesus used a play on words to emphasize the strength of the church that He was going to build. Many people today understand the church as a building. This is not the biblical understanding of church. The word *church* comes from the Greek word *ekklesia*, which is defined as "an assembly" or "called-out ones." So the root meaning of *church* is not that of a building but of people. Jesus said, "I will build My Church," which refers to a "new community" of people.

The Significance of the Day of Pentecost and the Church (Acts 2)

The outpouring of the Spirit, which initiated the church, occurred at Pentecost. Before His ascension into heaven, Christ commanded His disciples to wait at Jerusalem to receive the promise of the Father, saying, "You will be baptized with the Holy Spirit not many days hence" (Acts 1:5b). The Lord Jesus, after His earthly ministry, ascended to the right hand of the Father; but in a real sense He is still in the world manifested through His body, the church. It is of vital importance that we understand this metaphor of the church. We are always referring to the church in terms of its buildings. However, in reality, the church buildings simply house the congregations designated by Christ as His body representing Him and ministering for Him on the earth. The apostle Paul expresses this relationship as follows: "And He (Christ) has put all things under his feet, and gave him to be the HEAD over all things to the church; which is his BODY, the fullness of him that fills all in all" (Eph. 1:22–23). Jesus returned to the Father, but before he left He promised, "Lo I am with you always." He is with us, as a head is with a body. He is still working on earth more powerfully than before (John 14:12). The members of His church are His arms, legs, and mouth. Jesus expressed this relationship with a different metaphor in John 15:5: "I am the vine, you are the branches: he that abides in me, and I in Him, the same brings forth much fruit: for without me you can do nothing."

I have deliberately taken time to give this brief account to encourage you to realize that all the actions taken by Christ should strengthen you in believing that God is for us in Christ. We are His body as believers in His work and mission. It is important that our purpose is to reveal that God is for us as evidenced throughout the history of the church, in and through the events toward the end of the age and the future coming of the Lord Jesus Christ. The many events that we as Christians experience progressively year after year, along with the world at large, continue to convince us that God is for us!

We cannot possibly cover all the historical events that took place; therefore, I have chosen those events that reveal the most evidence of God's work in the world toward our future with Him. Hopefully, you will be greatly encouraged to see that God is always working on behalf of His creation and His church, established through His Son Jesus Christ.

My Personal Experience Receiving the Baptism of the Holy Spirit

I was raised in a liturgically oriented church from a child. My mother was very devoted to the church and desired the same for us. However, when World War II began, I enlisted in the US Navy. Church had no relevance for me during that time. Upon my discharge, I decided to stay in California and establish a new life. I soon became acquainted with a family through their daughter, whom I had met at a skating rink, and she invited me to meet her parents. They were very gracious in helping me get established by helping me secure some employment. They offered a spare room temporarily until I could eventually find my own residence. As it turned out, I attended a charismatic church with them which at first was a very traumatic experience in comparison to my prior liturgically oriented church experience. After a few Sunday services, I became very comfortable and enjoyed the friendly congregation. On one particular Sunday the pastor preached a salvation message, and I began to experience an awareness that God was dealing with my heart. I became so fearful that I proceeded to leave the church building. A young lady who assisted the pastor was greeting people at the exit at this time. When she took my hand, she said, "I think God is speaking to you!" I replied, crying, "I don't know?" Immediately, two gentlemen took me to the altar and prayed with me, and at that moment I experienced the Spirit of God—and I was gloriously saved!

Eventually I became very active in the church as their head usher. It wasn't long before I invited the daughter, Nell Ann, of the family I was staying with to be my wife. She accepted, and the pastor performed the wedding ceremony. We were both active in the church. One particular Sunday, the church invited an evangelist to conduct extended revival services. In one of the services, he devoted time to introducing the subject "Baptism of the Holy Spirit." He clearly explained that this was an experience that God provided in conjunction with the indwelling of the Holy Spirit, in which He develops our Christian virtues or character, called the fruit of the Spirit—love, joy, peace, patience, kindness and goodness, faithfulness, meekness, and self-control. In contrast, the "Baptism of the Holy Spirit" is the empowerment of the Holy Spirit to do ministry under His anointing. I personally was very timid about expressing my faith. That night when the evangelist placed his hand on my head, I experienced the presence and power of the Holy Spirit, and I went all over the church speaking in other tongues, hugging people, and sensing the fullness of God. Both my wife and I received this experience and eventually served as evangelists and later established churches. This again gave evidence that God is for us!

In 1950 I enrolled in L.I.F.E. Bible College in California to become an ordained minister. At my graduation I became concerned because, in every previous graduation, the graduates were gathered on the platform to stand in a large circle. Members of the faculty would proceed to lay their hands on the heads of the graduates, and they would fall backward on the floor verbally praising God. I was very concerned because I knew that a number of them had fallen down reluctantly because they didn't want to appear that they were not anointed. I always had difficulty with this practice, and I was determined that I would not fall down. I decided to remain standing. I closed my eyes, lifted my hands, and sensed the presence of a faculty member, but I didn't feel him touching my forehead. When I opened my eyes, I found myself on my back on the floor; I had been moved by the Spirit of God and openly praised the presence of God in tongues. I never questioned God's desire to move in my life to this very day. I realized again how *God is for us,* demonstrating His power in and through us. These experiences are not simply results of our own ability or figments of our imagination but of God's desire and ability.

Part 3

Evidence That God Is for Us in the Church Age

Chapter 13

God Holds the Future

The coming of Pentecost and the miraculous outpouring of the Holy Spirit was evidenced by tongues of fire coming upon the disciples in the upper room, and they moved out to the gathering crowd who had filled Jerusalem in celebration of Pentecost, which occurred fifty days after the Passover Sabbath (Lev. 23:15-16; Acts 2). It was one of the three great festivals that Jewish people celebrated in Jerusalem, and the city was filled with Jews from every nation. Many gathered to witness this miracle of disciples speaking in various language dialects as a wonderful work of God. They immediately cried out, "What does this mean?" The apostle Peter came forward and explained what was happening by saying, "This is that the Prophet Joel prophesied of this coming of the Holy Spirit" (Acts 2:16). They were all amazed, and Peter proceeded to preach about Joel's message, explaining the whole issue concerning Jesus's life, His miracles, and His final crucifixion followed by His resurrection. He now sits at the right hand of the Father (place of power and authority) and will deal with His enemies. When they heard this, they cried, "What shall we do?" Peter immediately said to them,

> Repent, and let every one of you be baptized in the name of Jesus Christ for the remission of your sins; and you shall receive the gift of the Holy Spirit. For the promise is to you and to your

children, and all who are afar off as many as the
Lord our God will call. (Acts 2:38–39)

Those who received his words were baptized; and that day about three thousand souls were added. They joined with the teaching of the apostles and the fellowship, breaking of bread, and prayers. The scriptures say, "Then fear came upon every soul and many signs and wonders were done through the apostles. Now all who believed were together, and had all things in common. They sold their possessions and goods, and divided them among all, to anyone who had need" (Acts 2:43–47). Thus, the church was born and began to spread and grow to many parts of the Roman Empire. Christianity would now move to the ends of the earth, bringing many to Christ through the church. The church began to grow and to fulfill the Great Commission that Jesus gave to His disciples, as follows:

Then the eleven disciples went to Galilee, to the mountain where Jesus had told them to go.... Then Jesus came to them and said, "All authority has been given to Me in heaven and on earth. Go therefore and make disciples of all the nations, baptizing them in the name of the Father, and of the Son, and of the Holy Spirit, teaching them to observe all the things I have commanded you; and lo, I am with you always, *even to the end of the age.*" (Matt. 28:16, 18–20, emphasis added)

God intends to reach out to people of every tongue and nation and let them know that He loves them and desires to fill eternity with their presence. Once again we have great proof and assurance that God is for us and all who will believe.

In order to maintain our purpose, we cannot discuss much of the growth and development of the church at any length. However, there are important events that reveal and express how

God has continually shown His ultimate purpose for the gospel to be preached to the whole world, beginning at Jerusalem and moving into the non-Jewish world according to Acts 1:8: "You shall receive power when the Holy Spirit has come upon you and you shall be witnesses to Me in Jerusalem, and Samaria, and to the ends of the earth." The book of Acts, as recorded by the apostle Luke, serves as a bridge from the life of Christ to the church and its expansion from Jerusalem to the known world of that day. Christianity was to begin to move out into the non-Jewish world with the gospel message.

The Significance of Paul (formerly Saul of Tarsus) in God's Future Plan

Paul's life and ministry strongly reflect on our thesis that God is for us. Saul of Tarsus had become a full-time persecutor of the messianic Jews who became believers in Jesus. No one was yet called "Christian" but "people of the Way." Saul intended to arrest them and take them to Jerusalem, where the Sanhedrin had jurisdiction and they could be punished (Acts 9:2). Saul took letters to the synagogues of Damascus. (Keep in mind that these believers were still Jews.) The persecution intensified with the death of Stephen, who was a Hellenist—that is, a Greek- speaking Jew who embraced Christianity (Acts 6). He was arrested and brought before the Sanhedrin, who accused him of blasphemy. The scriptures explain that Stephen was a man "full of faith and power and did great wonders and signs among the people" (Acts 6:7–8). Stephen found himself in the middle of a conflict between the Jews who still embraced the Jewish culture and those who had turned more toward the Greeks in their language and culture. The Sanhedrin became furious about his sermon declaring that Jesus Christ was the true Messiah. This resulted in their stoning Stephen. His death eventually set into motion the thrust of evangelism beyond

Jerusalem and the biblical world. In Acts 8:1–3, we discover that Saul was standing by, consenting to Stephen's death, and at that time, he became a leader in the great persecution taking place. He made great havoc of the church, entering homes and dragging out both men and women, committing them to prison. Where was God at this time? Don't despair! None of this was unnoticed by God, and as you will see, He intervened to accomplish His purpose for us.

In a sense, God was indicating, "Saul, I've had enough of you and your hostility under the guise that you are protecting Me!" Saul posed as a very devout Jew and even expressed his credentials, stating, "I am a Pharisee, the son of a Pharisee!"

However, this whole scenario moves to Saul's dramatic conversion to Christ on the way to Damascus (Acts 9). His life is completely turned around from being the aggressive and zealous Pharisee against Christianity to a zealous apostle for Christ! Never underestimate the power and concern of God for His love and mission. Nothing is impossible with God. Think of it—this persecutor turned into one of the great leaders of Christianity. His extensive missionary journeys recorded throughout the book of Acts and his prolific thirteen epistles in the Bible powerfully demonstrate God's wisdom and power that can change lives. It certainly demonstrates that God is with us, protecting us and our future in Christ.

God's Work through the Apostle Peter to the Gentile World (Acts 10, 11)

Since the Gentiles did not know the good news and since the apostle Peter, steeped in Jewish Christianity, was not yet prepared to minister Christ to such people, God had to take the initiative. He had to deal with Peter about this. May I remind you again that all these incidents that I am bringing before you are to help you understand, through the scriptures, that God's overall purpose is for people to know His love and that He is always for them. We need to be reminded that the central theme of the book of Acts is found in chapter 1, verse 8:

> But you shall receive power when the Holy Spirit
> has come upon you; and you shall be witnesses to
> me in Jerusalem, and all Judea and Samaria, *and*
> *to the ends of the earth.* (emphasis added)

The following scenario demonstrates that God is always working His will and purpose. Following the ministry of the apostle Paul, the whole scene moves from the Jewish culture to the Gentile culture to fulfill His desire for the whole world. In the tenth chapter of Acts, we witness an incident involving a man called Cornelius in the city of Caesarea, a Gentile city. Cornelius was a centurion of the Italian regiment. He would have been a captain of the Roman army in charge of a legion. It is significant that Cornelius was one who feared (revered) God with all his household. Those Gentiles who were most receptive to the gospel of Christ were called "God-fearers," such as Cornelius. He was a devout man in that he gave alms generously to the people and always prayed to God. On one occasion, while he was fasting and praying, he experienced a vision of an angel who spoke his name: "Cornelius!" He was afraid and responded, "What is it, Lord?" The angel answered, "Your prayers have been heard. Now send men to Joppa for Simon whose surname is Peter" (Acts 10:1–5). In the meantime we witness Peter's visit to the house of Simon, a tanner (Acts 9:43). A tanner was one of the most unclean trades in any ancient society. The nature of their work kept them in a state of ritual uncleanliness (Lev. 11:35), and the process of tanning leather resulted in a state of physical uncleanliness. My purpose in relating this detail is that Peter shared hospitality with an outcast. The fact that Cornelius, a Gentile, was directed to fetch Peter, a Jew, presents a problem. While those who were sent by Cornelius were on their way, Peter went up to the housetop to pray.

> While he was up there he became hungry, while they made ready, Peter fell into a trance and saw heaven opened and an object like a great sheet bound on four corners, descending to him and let down to the earth. In it were all kinds of four-footed animals of earth, wild beasts, creeping things, and birds of the air. And a voice came to him, "Rise, Peter; kill and eat." (Acts 10:10–13)

Peter refused, declaring that he had never eaten anything common or unclean. At that point, a voice spoke to him again, saying, "What God has cleansed you must not call common" (Acts 10:15).

I want to help you understand this situation. Peter had no problem staying in the home of a tanner who was unclean, yet he was about to enter the home of a Gentile God-fearer, someone who was likely more "clean" than the tanner with respect to the law. The difference, of course, is that even if Cornelius was a God-fearer, he was still an uncircumcised Gentile. This incident reveals quite well that God is for all people regardless of race, color, or creed, especially those who accept Him as their Savior. God prepared Peter to understand that what God has cleansed in their heart is to be accepted by all. Peter continued to travel to the house of Cornelius, but he still didn't quite get the point of his vision. The Spirit said to Peter to go with the men and not to doubt because God had sent them. Those sent by Cornelius arrived and invited Peter to accompany them and others to the house of Cornelius. On the next day Peter went away with them, and some brethren from Joppa accompanied him (Acts 10:17–23).

The Significance of the Meeting with Cornelius's Household (10:24–47)

Peter was told by the Spirit to go without misgivings. However, he took some brethren from Joppa with him. No doubt he wanted to have witnesses to corroborate his telling of the incident to the leaders in Jerusalem. Peter began to give a sermon in Acts 10:34–43, but he was interrupted as the Holy Spirit fell upon all those who believed. Peter laid his hands upon them that they might receive the gift of the Holy Spirit. But God interrupted this procedure because they were already yielding themselves to Him. It also gave Peter the assurance that God was receiving these Gentiles, as well as Jews, into the faith together. Read Acts 11:1–18 to see how Peter rehearses all this with the apostles and brethren in Judea and how they glorified God for His acceptance of the Gentiles into the faith. Now we have shown how God has been working throughout selected periods of biblical history, from the Old Testament and the New Testament, revealing that *God is for us and with us.* I have deliberately stopped at the point in the book of Acts that revealed how God united Jew and Gentile to create a church consisting of all those who believe and accept Jesus Christ as the Savior of the world. The word *church* in the Greek language is *ekklesia,* meaning "a called-out assembly or congregation." The church needs to see itself as being called out by God. Unfortunately, today we have confined ourselves to a church building where we attend, sing songs, pray, and hear a sermon followed by a benediction. The true image is a body of believers gathered together and representing themselves as the body of Christ, worshiping as disciples learning God's truth and going forth into their world seeking to disciple others for the kingdom of God. One of the best passages to show understanding of the church is found in Matthew 16:13–18.

When Jesus asked His disciples "Who do men say that I the Son of Man am?" they answered,

"Some say John the Baptist, some Elijah, and others Jeremiah or one of the prophets." Then He said to them, "But who do you say I am?" Simon Peter answered and said, "You are the Christ, the Son of the living God." Jesus answered and said to him, "Blessed are you Simon Bar-Jonah, for flesh and blood has not revealed this unto you, but My Father who is in heaven. And I also say unto you that you are Peter, and on this rock I will build My church, and the gates of Hades shall not prevail against it."

Jesus used a clever play on words to teach His disciples about the church. When Jesus referred to Peter by name (Greek *petros*), He used the word for a small, moveable stone. Jesus was saying that the church would not be built on Peter, the "pebble," but on Christ, the massive rock and cornerstone (Eph. 2:20). He was saying, in effect, that Peter's confession was the truth and that the church refers to a people who would constitute the body of Christ.

Chapter 14

The Development of the Church from AD 100–1517 and the Church under Roman Persecution (AD 100–313)

The Persecution of Christians

We will now proceed beyond the New Testament and pursue some of the decisive moments of the church age during the rule of the Roman Empire. The church went through heavy persecution and struggled for survival. This may cause you to question our thesis that God is for us since it appears that He was absent during this time. But that is not so. God is always active in His world, even though many different factors may seek to destroy His good works.

First, let's consider the basic causes of the persecution that Christians faced.

1. *Christian unpopularity because of intolerance.* They had religious differences with the culture of Rome and its pagan beliefs.
2. *Superstitions of pagans concerning calamities.* The Christians were blamed for insulting their gods and thus causing calamities.
3. *The government's interest in the revival of state religion.* Their morals and ethics were not based on salvation as the Christians' were.

4. *The refusal of Christians to participate in emperor worship.*
    This was difficult to avoid. It would require lip service,
    which Christians could not do in good conscience and
    still obey Christ. Various Roman emperors were involved
    throughout this period, but for our purposes, I am going
    to give attention to how God intervenes in this period with
    the reign of Constantine, who was in power until 337.

The Church of the Age of Constantine (AD 313–600)

The Emperor Constantine's Conversion and the Triumph of Christianity

Constantine was the first Roman emperor to embrace
Christianity. But as a man he's a historical enigma, and a great
deal of conflicting information surrounds him. What matters is
that he converted to some sort of Christianity at a point in his
life. The story goes that he had a vision of the cross before one
of the crucial battles in the civil wars that brought him to power,
and on this cross was written, "With this ensign, conquer!"
According to later legend, this became his royal insignia, and
consequentially Christianity had won itself an emperor. Whatever
really happened, this emperor's adoption of Christianity stopped
the persecution of Christians once and for all. He created the
Edict of Milan in 313. He did not go so far as to declare Rome a
Christian state, but he did enforce a policy of official neutrality
in Christian affairs. Under his regime, Christians were free at
least to speak as themselves in public without fear of reprisal or
torture and, more importantly, to worship as they wished. There
is much more information about his involvement in some of the
church issues of that day. But for our purpose in presenting
some of this historic information, we are interested in pointing
out how God is for His church in every generation and will
fulfill His purpose to the end of time. (This information about
Constantine was taken from online course information titled

"Early Christianity and the Church," History and Civilization by Mark Damen, 2016).

The Church of the Dark Ages or Middle Ages (AD 600–1517)

The Dark Ages are commonly known as the early part of the Middle Ages. Often the term *Dark Ages* refers to the initial five hundred years following the fall of Rome in 476. They are believed to have begun around AD 450 and continued until AD 1000. Is there any evidence that God was active during this period of time? Certainly, Christianity suffered some setbacks. The seeming triumph of Christianity was due to the fact that its adherents professed allegiance to the Roman Empire, not realizing that it would become a major threat. This resulted in a large proportion of those who bore the Christian name to compromise with the non-Christian environment in which they were immersed (Latourette, 1953, 269–270).

It often appears that the church and its message in its history were losing hope. Throughout the centuries, God has preserved His Word and raised up individuals for the task. Though the truth of the gospel was available in the Roman Catholic Church and Holy Roman Empire when it was at the height of its power, a common-language Bible was being suppressed; however, even then, God's people were active. God's hand is never "shortened that it cannot save" (Isa. 59:1). Even in the darkest hour of the church, God is present. It is beyond our purpose here to express all the details of the events of this period, which lasted many years (AD 450 to AD 1000). Remember, our overall purpose is to reveal that God is always in control and preserving His church and His people throughout history.

The Lutheran and Calvinistic Reformation Leading to a New World History (AD 1517 to the Present)

Here we have two real champions of the Protestant faith. While there were others who contributed to this great moment in history, Martin Luther and John Calvin give us an adequate understanding of this period in history that moved Christianity into the modern world. Our purpose is to give a brief overview of these particular historic events to reveal how God works to show that He is for us collectively as well as individually. These will constitute only a basic overview since these periods are very detailed and go beyond our purpose. Many causes contributed to the need for reformation. Abuses in the papacy over a period of time laid a foundation. Worldliness of the church was evident as priests and bishops entered their positions for money. Many would farm out their parishes to seminary students and go fishing. This period is very expansive and complicated. The events of history are always progressive and complicated, even in our present day. However, I can assure you that God's all-seeing eyes are active and knowledgeable about all events. My intent is to encourage you to have faith in the God of the universe, who is always active and moving circumstances into His perfect will and purpose. Here we witness the emergence of an expanding, dynamic world. By 1500, the foundations of the old medieval society were breaking up, and a new society with a larger geographic horizon—with changing political, economic, intellectual, and religious patterns—was slowly coming into being. The changes were revolutionary, both in their scope and in their effects upon the social order (Cairns 1954, 297).

A Brief Background of Martin Luther's Monastic Life

(Note: The following material has been adapted in part from seminary class notes taught by my church history professor, Dr. James Christian, in 1956–57).

There were many reformers rising to the occasion, but they were unsuccessful in bringing reform to the medieval Roman Catholic Church from within its system. Earlier, men attempted to reform some of the issues prevailing in the church; however, it appears that Martin Luther proved to be God's man during this time. Luther's childhood home was one of medieval Catholic piety. His parents were faithful, devoted members of the church. What constituted such a home?

1. Children were taught the Ten Commandments, the Lord's Prayer, and some simple hymns and chants.
2. They were taught that the emperor was God's ruler on earth, that the church was the house of the pope, and that the pope was God's representative on earth.
3. They also heard much about the devil and the evil spirits that filled the air, the water, the forests, and the mountains and valleys and did great harm to the people and to their cattle.

This early training left deep impressions on the mind and spirit of young Luther. Following several narrow escapes from death, and several other impressive personal experiences, he had a desire to become a monk, this being the highest form of holy life he knew to follow. Soon he entered a monastery of the Augustinian Order, known for their strict rules and cultivation of theological learning. It is not our intent to elaborate on the total life of Luther because our purpose is to observe how God used him to release the church from its bondage within the Roman Catholic religious abuses of that time. Here again, we see how God intervenes for people of faith to show that He is for them and will not tolerate any system or person that deters them from His purpose for their life. I want you to take note of how God's providence was directing Martin Luther's steps. He eventually entered a monastery of the Augustinian Order, and in 1507, he was ordained and celebrated his first mass. Later during the winter of 1508, he taught theology one semester at a new university that had been founded in Wittenberg by Frederick, the Elector of Saxony. His studies were mainly theological and only made his soul struggle more intensely, but he found some help from the godly Staupitz, the vicar general of his order, who urged him to trust God and to study the Bible. On one occasion, he was sent to Rome on business for his order. There he saw something of the corruption and luxury of the Roman Church and came to realize the need for reform. Eventually, Luther was transferred to Wittenberg, became a professor of Bible, and received his doctor of theology degree. He began to lecture in the vernacular on the books of the Bible and gradually developed the idea that only in the Bible could true authority be found. He lectured on Psalms, Romans, Galatians, and Hebrews. While preparing these lectures, he found peace in his soul that he had not been able to find in rites, acts of asceticism, or the mystics. A reading of Romans 1:17 convinced him that only faith in Christ could make one just before God. It was his study of the Bible that led him to trust Christ alone for his salvation (Cairns 1954, 313–315).

In 1517 Tetzel, the agent of the Archbishop Albert, began his sale of indulgences near Wittenberg. Tetzel claimed that repentance was not necessary for the buyer of an indulgence and that the indulgence gave complete forgiveness of all sin. This infuriated Luther, and he condemned the abuses of the indulgence system and challenged all comers to debate the matter. That same year, Luther posted his Ninety-Five Theses on the door of the church in Wittenberg. Here again, in a very crucial time in history, God raised up the man, Luther, much like He had done throughout biblical history. We must always believe that God is for us, His people, in every generation. Luther did not take his challenge lightly. He knew that He was obeying God's will and purpose. Luther had entered what was called the religious life because he was worried about his own relationship with God. The more he got to know the Church from the inside, the more he felt that the Church was not really being helpful in relating people to God. His challenge in the Ninety-Five Theses caused the pope and other members of the hierarchy to propose that he be excommunicated from the Church as a heretic. In 1521 he was summoned to appear before the Diet (or Assembly) to the Roman Empire. There he still insisted on the right to make up his own mind as to the meaning of the Bible, and he was condemned and made an outlaw. A number of events followed Luther's excommunication that forced him to develop a church organization and liturgy suitable for his followers. An assembly in 1529 declared that the Roman Catholic faith was the only legal faith. The princely followers of Luther read a "Protestation," and from then on they were known as Protestants by their opponents. Such was the honored derivation of the word *Protestant* (Cairns 1954, 320).

The Important Systematizer of Protestant Theology: John Calvin (1509–1564)

> While Luther was the daring trailblazer for the movement, Calvin was the careful thinker who bound the various Protestant doctrines into cohesive whole. Luther's tortured quest for salvation and his joyous discovery of justification by faith were such that they always dominated his theology. Calvin, as a theologian of the second generation, did not allow the doctrine of justification to eclipse the rest of Christian theology, and therefore was able to pay more attention to several aspects of the Christian faith that Luther had almost ignored. (Gonzalez, 1984, 61)

John Calvin, who spent most of his life in Geneva, France, was without a doubt the most important systematizer of Protestant theology of the sixteenth century. Unlike Luther, Calvin was born into the church. His father was an administrative assistant for the bishop of that time. Calvin was much younger than Luther. Both men studied law, with Calvin graduating and Luther forgoing finishing law school to become a monk and eventually a doctor of theology. Thanks to Luther's passion as the first generation of the Protestant Reformation, Calvin inherited a rich theological legacy, which he was able to cultivate. These two great men added to all those throughout biblical history who moved us forward into the modern world and directed its history to our ultimate end in the eternity in Jesus Christ, our Lord and Savior. I want to explain that our treatment of these two great leaders affirmed, in a great way, our thesis throughout this book that God is for us! Many leaders who were part of the growing reformation period reinforced the fact that God was moving history toward the modern new world. We will deal with this as we continue to explore the presence and work of God in behalf of our future.

Let me just list these reformers to give you a sense of how God was moving in the world:

- In Germany: Martin Luther
- In Switzerland: Ulrich Zwingli
- In France: John Calvin
- In England: John Wycliffe
- In Bohemia: John Huss
- In Prussia: Ludwig von Zinzendorf
- In the Netherlands: William of Orange
- In Scotland: John Knox

All these men were instrumental in the process of moving the message of God into the modern world. We need to have faith that God is in control of history. In fact someone made the observation that history is really "His story"!

The Invention of the Printing Press for the New World

Johannes Gutenberg (c. 1398–1468) invented the printing press in the 1450s, and the first book to ever be printed was a Latin language Bible, printed in Mainz, Germany. I believe this was inspired by God in order for the New World to have His Word in the language of the people from that point on. Interesting enough, Martin Luther immediately had a copy printed in German. This printed Bible opened the door to spread Christianity to the New World. It became evident that God is for His world and its people.

General Divisions of Church History

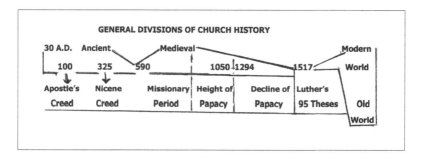

Part 4

Evidence That God Is for Us in the New World

As we now will consider the modern period to the end of the age, we will use a different format by dealing with issues that developed throughout the New World. The various historical developments until the end of human history continue to reveal how God is for us and thus gives us eternal hope that will not end. We are looking forward to the second coming of Christ and the rapture of the body of believers into eternity, where life will never again pose the question of whether God is for us. In the modern period of history, we will witness many contributions and developments that will strengthen our assurance that God's providence has been guiding the events of history until the end. I am convinced that we currently moving rapidly toward what the Bible refers to as "the last days," but we take heart that in the light of this truth, it is evident that God is and will be in control.

Let us consider the development of the Bible for the modern period of history that made the scriptures available to us until the end of the age and the second coming of Jesus. In God's providence He made sure that His Word would be available to all people. Our focus here is basically on the history of the English Bible. However, in the centuries that followed, the Bible was translated into the languages of many cultures of the world. God is using the ministry of the Wycliffe Global Alliance to accomplish this today. It is amazing how God has inspired and used this untiring ministry to produce the scriptures in the languages of the various cultures. This ministry was started by a missionary named William Cameron Townsend. He was shocked when he realized that many people could not understand the books of the Bible, so he started a linguistics school that trained students to do Bible translations. Over the decades from 1951 to today, they have translated the Bible into many languages, and their goal is to translate the Bible into every language by 2025. Here is more evidence that God is for the peoples of the world.

The development of the Bible for the modern period of history made the scriptures available to us until the end of the age and the second coming of Jesus.

History of the English Bible

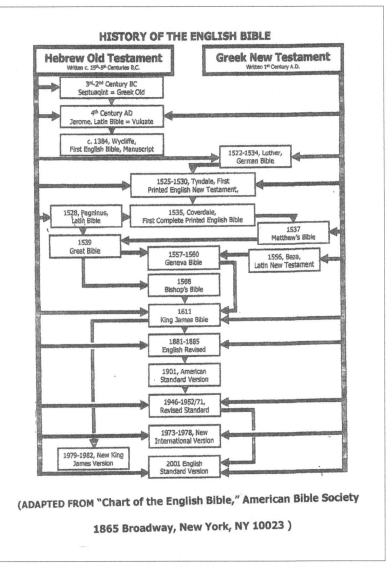

HISTORY OF THE ENGLISH BIBLE

Hebrew Old Testament
Written c. 15th-5th Centuries B.C.

Greek New Testament
Written 1st Century A.D.

3rd-2nd Century BC
Septuagint = Greek Old

4th Century AD
Jerome, Latin Bible = Vulgate

c. 1384, Wycliffe,
First English Bible, Manuscript

1522-1534, Luther,
German Bible

1525-1530, Tyndale, First
Printed English New Testament,

1528, Pagninus,
Latin Bible

1535, Coverdale,
First Complete Printed English Bible

1537
Matthew's Bible

1539
Great Bible

1557-1560
Geneva Bible

1556, Beza,
Latin New Testament

1568
Bishop's Bible

1611
King James Bible

1881-1885
English Revised

1901, American
Standard Version

1946-1952/71,
Revised Standard

1973-1978, New
International Version

1979-1982, New King
James Version

2001 English
Standard Version

(ADAPTED FROM "Chart of the English Bible," American Bible Society

1865 Broadway, New York, NY 10023)

(Adapted from "Chart of the English Bible," American Bible Society, New York, NY)

Chapter 15

The Renaissance Period

During the close of the Middle Ages a new enthusiasm for learning sprang up in Italy that came to be known as the Renaissance ("New Birth"). There was a renewed interest in classical literature, education, and art. During the course of the fifteenth and sixteenth centuries a new culture evolved in Europe. Using the word in a somewhat broader sense, we may define the Renaissance as the reentrance into the world of the secular, inquiring, self-reliant spirit that characterized the life and culture of classical antiquity. This is simply to say that under the influence of this intellectual revival the men of Western Europe came to think and feel beyond themselves to look inquiringly upon life and the outer world ... *they ceased to think and feel as mediaeval men and began to think and feel as modern men.* (emphasis added; Van Ness Myers 1905, 251 ff)

It is important to see that the Renaissance and the Reformation contributed to the creation of an ethic of individual dualism. Thus, the modern era opened the way for the individual's rights and responsibilities to interpret scripture according to the dictates of his or her conscience, not those determined by the church. In other words, understanding the Bible was inspired by the Spirit to the believer's heart. The Bible was not available to common people in medieval times (fifth–fifteenth centuries), but this was a serious matter. God intended that His Word would be available to all people to reveal His truth and that truth would set them free from this world's difficulties and hindrances. Again, God is continually for us in every stage of history.

Our purpose from this point is to emphasize how the modern period afforded the Bible and further implications and benefits of its availability to every individual who desired to procure one. As we proceed through this modern period you will experience in full measure how God is for us and has supplied all that we need to secure our eternal destiny with Him.

Why was the Bible not available to the common people in the medieval period? I would like to give the following plausible reasons:

1. The common people were poor and could not afford to get a Bible.
2. The Bible was not for sale in the common markets.
3. The Catholic Church did not want the common people to read the Bible.
4. Many of the common people were illiterate.
5. Most people had the mind-set that reading the Bible was the job of scholars.

Such a dilemma required the initiative of learned men to begin to correct the situation in order that the population would be able to take advantage of the holy writings.

The Reformers immediately faced challenges. Having argued that scripture is the ultimate authority in matters of truth and practice, thus elevating it over human institutions, the Reformers trusted the same Holy Spirit who would lead the Christians to a correct interpretation of scripture. This evoked the need for readable and organized Bibles for the common people to be able to read and understand the meaning under knowledgeable teachers and scholars.

To this day we find it almost impossible to think of the Christian faith without the Bible. When we look back over Christian history, we find few, if any, decisions more basic than those made during the first three centuries surrounding the formation of the Bible. The scriptures served not only as the inspiration for believers facing martyrdom but as the supreme standard for the churches threatened by heresy.

For our purposes I have chosen to give our attention to the English versions created throughout the centuries. When Latin was no longer the universal language of Europe, common people could no longer read the Bible; actually, the Bible was read to the people by the scholars and priests of the Catholic Church.

The English Translations through the Centuries (see chart p. 71)

- *The Wycliffe Bible, 1382 (prior to the Reformation):* John Wycliffe was an Oxford scholar who translated the Vulgate (Latin) into English. He was condemned as a heretic. Further unauthorized translations were forbidden under the penalty of excommunication.
- *The Tyndale Bible, 1525–1531:* William Tyndale, Oxford scholar, translated the New Testament from Greek and part of the Old Testament from Hebrew. It was printed in Germany because of England's opposition to the text's "heretical" slant.
- *The King James Bible, 1611:* King James ordered a new version, accomplished by fifty scholars working together. This is a Bible of great beauty and power that significantly influenced the English language and has been a standard for many years.

Today many translations continue to be made available in an effort to make the Bible more understandable for everyone. The following are some examples of popular newer versions to make the Bible easier to read and understand:

- American Standard Version (ASV), 1901
- Revised Standard Version (RSV), 1971
- New International Version (NIV), 1973

Just consider how fortunate we are to have the possibility of every person living in the modern world today possessing the Word of God. Establishing access to the Word of God further enforces our thesis that God is for us in every generation. The Bible is God's book now available for us.

The Bible is a unique, redemptive book. God is not willing that any should perish. This has been God's desire from the beginning of Creation. Consider the following scriptures.

> For God so loved the world that He gave His only begotten Son, that whoever believes in Him should not perish but have everlasting life. For God did not send His Son into the world to condemn the world, but that the world through Him might be saved. (John 3:16–17)

> My sheep hear My voice, and I know them, and they follow Me. And I give them eternal life, and they shall never perish; neither shall anyone snatch them out of My hand. (John 10:27–28)

> All scripture is given by inspiration of God, and is profitable for doctrine, for reproof, for correction, for instruction in righteousness, that the man of God may be complete, thoroughly equipped for every good work. (2 Tim. 3:16)

> The Lord is not slack concerning His promise, as
> some men count slackness, but is long-suffering
> toward us, not willing that any should perish but
> that all would come to repentance. (2 Peter 3:9)

These are only a few of the scriptures that give us assurance of God's love and devotion to His creation. When the Bible became available to the post–Reformation generation, it gave a greater opportunity to strengthen people's faith by creating the system of theology for their benefit and that of future generations.

Chapter 16

<hr>

The Need for a Development
of Biblical Theology

As more people began to acquire the scriptures for their enlightenment and use, it was necessary to establish a system of theology to help them understand the proper application of scripture to everyday life and its meaning. Biblical theology attempts to arrange the doctrines of the Bible according to their historical background, in contrast to systematic theology, which categorizes doctrine according to specific topics. Biblical theology shows the unfolding of God's revelation as it progressed through history. Consider the following reasons biblical theology was necessary at this time.

1. *The unity of the church demanded it.* Remember, the people were not used to having access to the scriptures, and they needed help in understanding them. This would require recognized, qualified teachers among them, similar to what took place in the Old Testament and the early church. In the Old Testament (Neh. 8:8), the leaders "read from the book, from the Law of God, clearly, and they gave the sense, so that the people understood the reading." In the New Testament (1 Corin. 15), Paul refers to the tradition they had received from him. God has always given his people teachers to not only read scriptures but to communicate and guard the truth of scripture.

2. *Our view of scripture demanded it.* All of scripture is breathed out by God (2 Tim. 3:16). This means that everything in the Bible matters. It also means that everything in the Bible possesses a fundamental unity, coming as it does from the same author. Systematic theology seeks to make such comprehensive unity seen.
3. *The Bible's interest in truth demands it.* Systematic theology is nothing if not the pursuit of truth, which is essential to biblical Christianity. The Holy Spirit is called the Spirit of truth (John 14:17), and the work of the Holy Spirit was to guide the apostles into all truth (John 16:13).

It is to our advantage to understand how God is continually working His will in history. As we are moving through the great issues being directed by God in these latter times, may it continue to be an encouragement that He is for us and our eternal destiny. We have seen that God made it possible for the Bible to be accessible to all people. This was followed by the necessity of developing a systematic theology to unify the truth of the scriptures. The miracle of the Bible, which was protected through the Dark Ages and through the conflicts of many generations, is that we may have it today. It is not by chance that we have the Bible in our time. Devoted individuals like Martin Luther, John Wycliffe, William Tyndale, John Calvin, John Huss, and others diligently were moved to preserve the scriptures. God has ordained that His Word was to be proclaimed throughout the world. This was vitally important in the early church following the outpouring of the Holy Spirit at Pentecost, as told in the book of Acts. Jesus said,

> Go therefore and make disciples of all nations,
> baptizing them in the name of the Father, and of
> the Son, and of the Holy Spirit, teaching them to
> observe all things I have commanded you; *and lo,*

I am with you always even to the end of the age. Amen. (Matt. 28:19, emphasis added)

You shall receive power when the Holy Spirit has come upon you; and you shall be witnesses to Me in Jerusalem, and in all Judea and Samaria, *and to the end of the earth.* (Acts 1:8, emphasis added)

And the gospel must first be preached to all nations. (Mark 13:10)

God is determined to have the gospel preached in these last days until He comes. This is to assure us that the scriptures are secure today and to comfort us in the knowledge that God is for us, even until the end of time.

Chapter 17

Bible and Theology Prompted the Development of Preaching

There was a need to develop a system of preaching that would give credence to the scriptures and the resulting theology that was being established. Not having the scriptures taught with sufficient understanding would include a certain degree of danger. Proper preaching with understanding and application was crucial at this time. The apostle Paul admonished others about this earlier in 2 Timothy 4:2–4:

> Preach the Word! Be ready in season and out of season. Convince, rebuke, exhort, with all long-suffering and teaching. For the time will come when they will not endure sound doctrine but according to their own desires, because they have itching ears, they will heap up to themselves teachers; they will turn their ears from the truth, and be turned aside to fables.

God is very jealous about His Word being directed to the heart of the listener because it is His truth and He wants to make sure that people know that He is for them and keep them directed to His will and purpose. This is only possible if the Bible and true theology are preached with the anointing of the Holy Spirit. This was true for the preachers in the Apostolic Age, with the apostles Peter, Stephen, Philip, Timothy, Paul, Barnabas, and others; in the pre–Reformation Age, with men like John Wycliffe and John Huss; and in the Reformation with Martin Luther, Ulrich Zwingli, John Calvin, and John Knox. This became the criteria for those of the seventeenth, eighteenth, nineteenth, and twentieth centuries and today. Jay Adams says,

> There seems to be a direct relationship between the faithful preaching of the Word of God and the blessing on His Church. On the other hand, when the Word of God was not preached, the church began to grow obscure and out of step with the needs of the people (Adams 1974, 3).

The Place of Preaching in Scripture (1 Corin. 1:17–25)

The apostle Paul had to remind the Corinthian church as to what was the most important issue for the Church. The Corinthians were focused on the rite of baptism and needed to be reminded that it was a sign that acknowledged the work of Jesus Christ, His death, and His resurrection. Paul wrote,

> For Christ did not send me to baptize, but to *preach the Gospel* - not with words of human wisdom, lest the cross of Christ be emptied of its power. For *the message of the cross* is foolishness; to those who are perishing, but to us who are being saved it is the power of God. (1 Corin. 1:17-18, emphasis added)

Preaching is indispensable to Christianity. It has been the very essence of the Word of God being dispensed through the centuries. The living Word of God has revealed His person, love, and concern for fallen humanity. The Word of God is the greatest revelation that God is for us and not against us. God calls upon all who have heard and embraced His Word to speak it to others.

Preaching of the Old Testament Prophets

In the Old Testament God spoke through the prophets, admonishing and instructing His people, Israel. He commended them when they were obedient to His will but warned and instructed them when they strayed from it. Why was God so strict with them? Because God's purpose was to make them a conduit to distribute His redemptive will for all humanity and future generations.

Preaching of Jesus, the Apostles, and Church Fathers

Jesus

As we arrive at the New Testament we immediately see Jesus preaching; however, He was preceded by John the Baptist, his forerunner. But John the Baptist was primarily announcing the coming of Jesus. As we view the gospels, we discover that Mark was verifying the coming of the Messiah (Jesus). Jesus, the founder of Christianity, was one of its first preachers. Mark 1:14 states,

> Now after John was put in prison, Jesus came to Galilee, preaching the gospel of the kingdom of God, and saying, "The time is fulfilled, and the kingdom of God is at hand. Repent and believe in the gospel."

The Apostles

It is evident that, after Pentecost, the apostles gave priority to the ministry of preaching, which is specifically stated in Acts 6. The disciples were multiplying and so the Hellenists complained concerning the Hebrews' neglect of the widows in the daily distribution. The apostles resisted getting involved in the situation since they devoted themselves to prayer and to the ministry of the Word (Acts 6:4). They claimed that Jesus called them to preach (Mark 3:14–15). After the resurrection Jesus commissioned them to take the gospel to the nations (Matt. 28:19–20).

The Early Church Fathers

We find the same emphasis on preaching and teaching in the ministry of Jesus and His apostles as we find the among the early church fathers. It's not within the scope of our study to expound on all the history of the church fathers. Let it suffice to briefly mention the early church fathers who were within two generations of the twelve apostles of Christ. They were called the apostolic fathers since tradition describes them as having been taught by the twelve. Important apostolic fathers included such men as Clement of Rome, Ignatius of Antioch, Polycarp of Smyrna, and Papias of Hierapolis. They preached, defending the faith and teaching of the early church. Since the health of Christians and of the church depends on the Word of God, preaching and teaching is of utmost importance. This practice has continued to our present day. The Bible is our confidence in all things in this life and our life to come. We are charged to preach God's Word:

> I charge you therefore before God and the Lord Jesus Christ, who will judge the living and dead at His appearing and His kingdom: Preach the word. Be ready in season and out of season. Convince, rebuke, exhort, with all long-suffering and teaching. For the time will come when they will not endure sound doctrine, but according to their own desires, because they have itching ears, they will heap up to themselves teachers; and they will turn their ears away from truth,

and be turned away to fables.... Do the work of
an evangelist." (2 Tim. 4:2–5)

God has given this prime directive for us to proclaim His
Word at all costs, especially as the end of the age is looming on
the horizon. We must all be engaged in reaching others for Christ
before His coming!

> For the word of God is living and powerful, and
> sharper than any two-edged sword, piercing even
> to the division of soul and spirit, and of the joints
> and marrow, and is a discerner of the thoughts
> and intents of the heart. (Heb. 4:12)

God has provided everything that we need to maintain our
faith in Him. Once again, I emphasize that *God is for us in every
stage of our lives.*

> And my God shall supply all your needs according
> to His riches in glory by Christ Jesus. (Phil. 4:19)

God has inspired the ministry of preaching, and it is His will
that those who are called recognize that it is by the anointing
and power of His Spirit

God's Intervention That Changed My Vision of Ministry

It is so important that we trust in God completely and beware
of thinking that we can do our own thing, in our own strength.
I would like to share how God revealed this to me when I was in
Bible college, ready to embark on my ministry. I will never forget
how God dealt with me about my future. I had just finished my
classes for the day and was leaving for my part-time job that I
had that afternoon. I was running a little late to catch the trolley
to get to work. In order to save time I decided to take a shortcut

through the back of the large church that was connected to the Bible school. To my surprise, I was able to enter the building, and I wound my way around only to discover that it brought me out to the large church platform. I became overwhelmed by the enormous auditorium of several thousand seats. I had attended services there from time to time, but I had never viewed things from where I was standing on this platform. I suddenly was faced with the possibility of my preaching to a large crowd. I turned and sat in the large pulpit chair, and in my imagination I heard a voice saying, "And now ladies and gentlemen, I present to you the Reverend George P. Kimber!" I arose from the pulpit chair and headed toward the pulpit, and I was suddenly struck to my knees when I heard a voice saying, "They do not want to see or hear George P. Kimber. They want to see Jesus!" At that moment I saw inscribed on the back of the pulpit in gold letters, "We Would See Jesus!" I cried and asked for forgiveness. At that moment God supplied me with a scripture, 2 Corinthians 4:7, which says, "We have this treasure in earthen vessels, that the excellence of the power may be of God and not of us."

This became the foundation and goal of my ministry and teaching for over sixty years. I had a ring made with the scripture inscribed, and I wear it to this very day. I discovered that I needed this experience for the future ministry that God had ordained for me. In some way it reminded me of the experience of the apostle Paul in Acts 9 when he was on the Damascus Road, seeking to bring murderous threats against the Lord's disciples and asking for letters from the high priest to carry these threats out. I certainly am not comparing my incident with his, except it reinforced my determination to seek and do God's will and purpose in my life. This is my thesis for writing this book: that we need to reinforce that the scriptures reveal over and over that God is for us now and for eternity.

Chapter 18

==

The Ministry of Evangelism and Revival

Revival is not confined only to our modern periods of history. One of the most miraculous works of God in His world has been periods of declension followed by periods of revival. This is when God's Spirit moves people from destruction to redirect their lives to constructive, progressive living for God's purpose and ends. In modern times the term for *revival* is *awakening*, which is an appropriate term in comparison to being spiritually dead. We must be constantly reminded that God is always working, and we need to join Him in His work to find security for life now and the world to come. Christianity has always manifested itself in a mighty, dynamic way through the Holy Spirit. Many evangelistic movements were created over the last centuries and are increasing in our modern age. It would be impossible to trace many of these movements, but it seems quite evident that God has ordained that, in these last days, our world would experience the power and ministry of the Holy Spirit through increased evangelism and revivals before the second coming of Christ looming in the near future. Through history, revival has raised up key persons and movements across the world. I would call our attention to the Great Awakening of the eighteenth century, especially through Whitfield's evangelistic activity. The nineteenth century was strengthened by the work of great American evangelists such as Charles Finney and Dwight L. Moody and the outstanding work of Billy Graham's campaigns.

He preached to millions around the world. His ministry lasted for sixty-seven years of integrity while spreading the gospel. This is not an exhaustive treatment of evangelism. God cares for His world increasingly more in these last days and throughout all history. There is certainly a great need for a spiritual awakening in our growing modern society with its materialistic growth and people being lured into worldly things other than the spiritual, which invites them to future eternal things. If only our society would recognize that *God is for us* to help us be prepared for eternal life with Him.

There is a challenge before us to today to spread the gospel to the ends of the world. Wycliffe Global Alliance has been increasing their ability to translate the scriptures into as many languages as possible. Their development of new methods is showing promise.

Chapter 19

The Challenge of Modern World Missions

Consider the numerous people whom God has called to go into all the world to preach and minister the gospel. In most instances, their calls required not only training for the task but also the realization that God would be with them through all times and situations. Many times, their many tasks would seem impossible, but they would soon discern that God had gone before them and equipped them for the task. God never calls us to a task without equipping us and guiding us by His Holy Spirit. The condition of our world today is fulfilling the scriptural predictions of the last days. Consider the following:

> And this gospel will be preached in all the world as a witness *to all nations*, and then the end will come. (Matt. 24:14, emphasis added)

> But know this, that in the last days perilous times will come ... (2 Tim. 3:1)

> But the day of the Lord will come as a thief in the night, in which the heavens will pass away with a great noise, and the elements will melt with fervent heat; both the earth and the works that are in it will be burned up. (2 Peter 3:10–11)

God is very concerned about His world and has encouraged us do the work of evangelism while there is still time. He warns us in order to assure us those who put their trust in the gospel of the fact that Jesus is coming soon for those who have made themselves ready. Missions have greatly emphasized that God is for us to the end of history.

Consider the basis of missions found in the Great Commission declared by Jesus Christ in Matthew 28:16–18:

> The eleven disciples went into Galilee, to the mountain which Jesus appointed for them.... And Jesus came and spoke to them saying, "All authority has been given to Me in heaven and on earth. Go therefore and make disciples of all nations, baptizing them in the name of the Father and of the Son and of the Holy Spirit, teaching them to observe all things that I commanded you; and lo, I am with you always even to the end of the age."

This commission has not changed since the moment Jesus uttered it. Christians today are to go into all the world. Jesus wants us to reach beyond our boundaries and declare that God is for all people and He wants them as part of His eternal kingdom. Remember, as a Christian you are in His Kingdom now, waiting for the coming rapture of the church. We, the church, are basically God's colony on earth reaching out for others to join us. We are in the world but not really of the world. This world will one day pass away, along with all its corruption and rebellion, to God. That's why it is necessary for us to support and promote missions.

When we think of the Great Commission and its challenge to take the good news of the gospel to the utmost parts of the world, the immensity of it is staggering! But think of the underlying features within the Great Commission.

1. Jesus said, "All authority has been given to Me in heaven and on earth." There are no boundaries that can hinder His authority.
2. Therefore, we are commissioned to "make disciples of all nations." We are to be evangelists preaching the gospel or good news.
3. "Baptizing them in the name of the Father and of the Son and of the Holy Spirit" means that we must be aware that the disciples we make become the disciples of the Trinity, not us.
4. We are therefore commissioned "to teach them to observe the things that we were commanded to do." And we should not be apprehensive about this commission because God has promised, "Lo I am with you always, even to the end of the age."

One of the greatest attitudes that every Christian should develop is to never give up, regardless of the many situations that confront him or her. If there is one attitude that characterizes people of God in the Bible, it is perseverance. When we read about the many instances in the scriptures, though they often appear to be impossible, God always made a way out of the circumstances for His honor and glory and for the benefit of humanity. He would instill in them that their God is always for them. Hope is absolutely essential to life. The will to persevere is often the outgrowth of hope, and hope will not make us ashamed. We are faced with a world today that is full of violence, uncertainty, and political confusion—a world that is full of refugees seeking acceptance and new life. These phenomena are creating enormous difficulty for all of us. We need more than ever to take advantage of every opportunity to comfort and challenge those who are facing difficulties in life. We need to let them know there is a God who cares deeply for them and has done everything possible to help them in this life. We need to assure them that life does not end here. There is a great future in heaven that has been prepared through the redemptive work of Christ for whosoever will believe and accept Jesus Christ as their Lord and Savior now, today!

While we wait for heaven, consider how *God is for us* now. As we continue to move forward in this twentieth century and toward the future coming of Jesus Christ, let us be assured that God is for us now and until the end. "Jesus Christ is the same yesterday, today and forever" (Heb. 13:8).

Chapter 20

Issues of Our Present Day That Challenge Our Faith in God

We have been reviewing biblical history from the beginning to our present day. It is important that we accept the challenge of the issues of our present time and witness how God is with us and for us now. I would like you to consider several major situations in our world that challenge our faith and actions as Christians.

The Issue of Abortion

Abortion is one of the most controversial moral dilemmas of our day. Many women who experience unplanned pregnancy often see abortion as their only option. It is estimated that 40 percent of all pregnancies are unplanned, resulting in a staggering figure of at least two out of three unplanned pregnancies being terminated by abortion (US Department of Health and Human Services 1983). The most astounding report that I heard is that 1.6 million abortions are reported every year, meaning that over 40 million abortions have taken place since abortion was legalized in 1973. It is not our purpose here to discuss all the ramifications of abortion. The arguments for and against abortion are too voluminous to discuss or argue here. Our concern is to emphasize that *God is for us* in every situation in our lives. There are volumes of arguments regarding women's legal rights to various medical and scientific discussions. To think that the fetus is mere tissue and not a person shows little consideration for the biblical understanding of life from God's perspective. It is true that abortion is not a modern situation. History has revealed that it was a problem in many ancient societies, but we must not assume that it was ordained or approved by God. The Bible is silent about abortion. The reason is that it was unthinkable for an Israelite to consider that option. Children were viewed as a gift from God.

> Behold, children are a heritage from the Lord,
> the fruit of the womb is a reward. (Psa. 27:3).

One of the key passages revealing the sanctity of human life is Psalm 139:13–14:

> For you formed my inward parts; you covered
> me in my mother's womb. I will praise you, for
> I am fearfully and wonderfully made. (See also
> verses 15–16.)

I think our society has disregarded the importance of childbirth being a gift from God, and the church and Christianity itself needs to defend and plead for the right of children to be born under God's blessing and as His gift.

I would like to make you aware of an incident that occurred on February 3, 1994, at the annual National Prayer Breakfast in Washington, DC. Mother Teresa was invited to speak, and she talked about the dignity and value of life and the worthiness of all human life to be loved. Everyone gathered at the prayer breakfast could agree with that. But halfway through her talk she said,

> I feel that the greatest destroyer of peace today is
> abortion, because it is a war against the child, a
> direct killing of an innocent child, murder by the

mother herself. And if we accept that a mother can kill even her own child, how can we tell other people not to kill one another? And then, speaking directly into the room filled with some of the world's most powerful people, she pleaded,

Mother Terersa Before Congress and President Clinton

Please don't kill the child. I want the child. Please give me the child. I am willing to accept any child who would be aborted and to give that child to a married couple who will love the child and be loved by the child.... From our children's home in Calcutta alone we have saved over three thousand children from abortion. These children have brought such love and joy to their adopting parents and have grown up so full of love and joy.... If we remember that God loves us, and we can love others as He loves us, then America can become a sign of peace for the world. From here in Washington D.C., a sign of care for the weakest of the weak— the unborn child—must go out in the world. If you become a burning light of justice and peace in the world, then really you will be true to what the founders of this country stood for. God bless you!

February 3 1994 Prayer Breakfast

Mother Teresa spoke boldly to her elite audience that day, and they listened because she had earned the right to be bold. Everyone knew that Mother Teresa and her sister nuns walked their walk, caring for those the world has forgotten or chosen not to love. Let me emphasize that this is another example that God is for us and blesses those efforts that deliberately move to make things better in our world.

The Situation of Muslims Turning to Christ

For many years the Muslim world was definitely closed to the outside world. In fact, most people knew very little about them except for a few who scattered over years into other nations. Many have expressed skepticism as to how authentic these conversions are. We are talking about a large number of Muslims who live in various parts of the world. It is difficult to know if we can trust the fact that Muslims are turning to Christ. However, if they are authentic conversions, they may indicate that God is revealing that He is for them in these last days. Many of them are claiming to have visions of "Isa" (the Muslim name of Jesus). It is possible that the numerous people becoming refugees are more free to accept Christ without persecution. We realize the need for much caution from these reports since the purpose of some has been to deceive and achieve an underlying agenda. On the other hand, we need discernment to discover that God is working through His Spirit in many of these Muslim people, especially those who do not adhere to the more radical tenets of their religion. While the majority of the world's 1.5 billion Muslims want no part of the deadly violence and attempt to live in peace with their neighbors, the number of radicals who preach violence and terror is mushrooming around the world. I believe it is wise to be very cautious but at the same time discerning of how God is working with many in these last days.

Medical Advances in Our Day

During the life and ministry of Jesus Christ, He frequently ministered to and had compassion for the many physical needs of people. In fact, the apostle Luke was a physician, and Jesus's compassion is reflected over and over again in his gospel. It is amazing how Jesus revealed that God was for the afflicted both in body and soul. He also passed that on in the disciples' ministries.

It certainly seems obvious that God has made it possible for medical science to accomplish outstanding feats for humanity today. We are experiencing longer life spans and the unusual restoration of body parts, such as knee and hip replacements and pacemakers for unstable hearts, as well as more effective medicine for diseases such as diabetes, heart conditions, and those affecting other areas of the body. God has endowed doctors and physicians with greater skills, instruments, and procedures to help countless different patients today. The Bible declared in Daniel 12:4 that in the last days knowledge would be increased: "But you Daniel, shut up the words and seal the book until the time of the end; many shall run to and fro, and knowledge shall be increased."

My dear father worked very hard during the Depression years and eventually became very skillful in the shoe industry. However, he had a leaky valve in his heart that medical science was not yet advanced enough to treat. My father died at thirty-five years old. If he had lived into the future years of advance medicine procedures, he would have had additional years. We are blessed today because of advanced science.

I would certainly be remiss if I didn't recognize the increased humanitarian aid that has been provided to fulfill needs around the world. This includes such things as drilling wells for clean water and providing food, clothing, shelters, medical aid, and education. All this, I believe, is God's moving upon Christians to reach beyond their own borders and share their prosperity that they have received from God.

The Homosexual Dilemma

One of the most common clichés heard in homosexual circles is "Once gay, always gay." My purpose is not to debate the issue.

However, I have been concerned for those people struggling with homosexual feelings and feel that they cannot do anything about it. There are some groups like Exodus International that provide a network of organizations that specialize in helping homosexuals who are desperate to change their orientation. My purpose in addressing this situation is that I believe the Bible reveals scriptures saying that God is for them, meaning that there is deliverance for those who desire God's help. One of the most helpful portions of scripture is 1 Corinthians 6:9–11 (see also 1 Tim. 1:10):

> Do you not know that the unrighteous will not inherit the kingdom of God? Do not be deceived. Neither fornicators, nor idolaters, nor adulterers, nor homosexuals, nor sodomites, nor thieves, nor covetous, nor drunkards, nor revilers, nor extortioners will inherit the kingdom of God.

This is a very disturbing list of sins with which God is not pleased. However, verse 11 continues:

> And such were some of you. But you were washed, but you were sanctified, but you were justified in the name of the Lord Jesus and by the Spirit of our God.

Notice that here is continued evidence that God is for us in every situation of life!

The Need for Hope That God Is for Us in These Last Days

Certainly, we are becoming aware that our world is in great turmoil. There is increasing evidence of a restless world with intensifying terrorism and war everywhere. The present warfare and terrorism cannot be fought like the conventional warfare conducted in the past. In Matthew 24:6–8, Jesus said,

> Take heed that no one deceive you.... You will hear of wars and rumors of wars. See that you are not troubled; for all these things must come to past, but the end is not yet. For nation will rise up against nation, and kingdom against kingdom. And there will be famines, pestilence, and earthquakes in various places. All these are the beginning of sorrows.

These things are becoming more and more evident in our present day and will continue to escalate in the coming days and years. We need to take heart in God's sovereign presence in our world and universe. We must understand and believe that God is in control of our world and the universe. The Bible makes it very clear that in spite of all the upheaval in these last days, God is for us now and forever.

Chapter 21

Heaven: The Final Frontier of Our Christian Journey

Stepping from this earthly life into the glory of heaven will be one of the most glorious steps we will have made. Heaven is the most positive evidence in the Bible that God has been with us and will be with us for eternity. We have been witnessing throughout the scriptures how God continually intervened in biblical history's various difficult times from creation to the final book of Revelation. There are many who still question heaven as a reality. I want you to know that everlasting life is literal and tangible. When Jesus rose from the dead, he invited His followers to actually touch Him to show that He was not a figment of their imagination. It was as if Jesus was saying, "I am alive, I am real, and I will be eternally alive with you forever in heaven." This is our hope that will not pass away. It's real!

The Experience of the Death of My Father-in-Law

I was like a son to him, and he was as a father to me. My birth father died in his thirties, and my widowed mother never remarried. After my experience in the navy in World War II, I was discharged in Southern California and never returned to my home in Massachusetts. I eventually met a girl and her family, and they helped me get oriented back into life. In marrying their daughter and officially becoming a member of the family, my father-in-law, being a very active and successful blacksmith, invited me to join him and help him in his work. We became very close, and he became as a real father to me and considered me as a son more than a son-in-law. When He was suddenly was stricken physically and was at death's door, I was alone with him while the rest of the family was in the waiting room. He reached out and firmly took my hand, and suddenly he raised up with his other arm. With a smile and burst of joy, he shouted, "Well, glory to God!" Slowly he fell back in the bed and went to be with Jesus. I cherished that moment, and at the same time I realized how much of a real father he was to me. I know that God knew I needed a father to nurture me, which he did. I know my joy will be full when in heaven I will be with my birth father and my dear father-in-law as a blessed son!

Heaven Is a Real Place, Real People, Real Purpose

In our human imaginations, we try to speculate about heaven. The most ridiculous speculation is the notion that we will all be sitting on clouds strumming harps. It is very difficult to grasp the concept of heaven without the inspired Word of God and its truth and witness. Without such a source, we are left to or own imagination. Consider the follow evidence, both in logic and reality. Heaven was God's plan at creation before the fall of Adam and Eve. In Genesis 3, the serpent's (Satan) lie caused Adam and Eve to question God's purpose; thus, it resulted in their being condemned to physical and spiritual death. God determined to reverse this curse by pronouncing a covenant in Genesis 3:15. Speaking to the serpent (Satan), He said, "I will put enmity between you and the woman, and between your seed and her seed; it shall bruise your head, and you will bruise his heel." The coming of the woman's seed was fulfilled in Jesus's birth (Matt. 1–2; Luke 2; Gal. 4:4). On the cross, Jesus's body was bruised and broken; at the second coming, Satan's head will be bruised (Rom. 16:20). The victory through the cross and the resurrection restored God's promise of heaven for all believers in Jesus as their savior. Actually, for the believers in Christ, our heavenly life has already begun—when we received Christ by faith, the Holy Spirit entered our life and guaranteed eternal life. "God has put eternity in their hearts" (Ecc. 3:11). The purpose of heaven is to restore the glory of His creation so that "mankind might glorify God, and ... enjoy Him forever" (Westminster Catechism).

One of the most provocative books written about heaven is *Heaven* by Randy Alcorn (Carol Stream, Tyndale, 2004). I think it would be profitable to present some of the questions that his book answers in terms of what people are curious about when it comes to heaven. I will not present the full details of each question but just the basic idea.

What Will Our Lives Be Like? (pp. 273–331)

1. Will *we be o*urselves in *h*eaven? Continuity of identity ultimately requires a bodily resurrection. Unless we grasp the resurrection, we won't believe that we'll continue to be ourselves in the afterlife. We are physical beings. If the eternal heaven is a disembodied state, then our humanity will either be diminished or transcended and we will never again be ourselves after we die (p. 273). Job said, "In my flesh I will see God; ... I, and not another" (Job 19:26, 27). The risen Christ said, "Look at my hands and my feet. It is I myself! Touch me and see; a ghost does not have flesh and bones, as you see I have" (Luke 24:39).
2. Will we have emotions? (pp. 276– 277) In scripture, God is said to enjoy, love, laugh, take delight, and rejoice. We should consider that our emotions are derived from God's. In heaven we'll exercise not only intellect but also emotions (Rev. 7:11–12; 18:1–24). We know that people

in heaven have lots of feelings––all good ones. We're told of banquets, feasts, and singing. People will laugh there (Luke 6:21).

3. Will we maintain our own identities? (pp. 278– 279) You will be you in Heaven. Who else would you be? The resurrected Jesus did not become someone else; He remained who He was before the resurrection: "It is I myself!" (Luke 24:29).

4. Will our bodies be perfect? (p. 286) I often think of how paraplegics, quadriplegics, and people who have known constant pain will walk, run, jump, and laugh in the New Earth. Believers who are blind now will gawk at the New Earth's wonders. What a special pleasure for them.

Joni Eareckson Tada, a quadriplegic, was once quoted as saying,

> "I still can hardly believe it. I, with shriveled, bent fingers, atrophied muscles, gnarled knees, and no feeling from the shoulders down, will one day have a new body, light, bright, and clothed in righteousness—powerful and dazzling. Can you imagine the hope that gives someone spinal-cord injured like me? … No other religion, no other philosophy promises new bodies, hearts, and minds. Only in the gospel of Christ do hurting people find such incredible hope."… But then she added, "And you're going to get new minds." The class she was talking to broke out in cheers and applause. They knew just what they wanted— new minds.

It appeared that God was not ever going to improve Joni's bodily condition, but Joni's faith in God caused her to accomplish many things for Him in spite of her afflictions. Certainly, she will be completely whole and walking the streets of gold, laughing and praising God for His work that He accomplished through her life on earth. *God has been for her.*

These are just a few things that we can look forward to. There is a chorus about heaven we used to enjoy singing in my church. It goes like this: "Heaven is a wonderful place, full of glory and grace. I'm going to see my Savior's face. Heaven is a glorious, Heaven is glorious, Heaven is a glorious place." I don't think we realize how much God has done through His Son, Jesus Christ, to guarantee our future destiny. It will take an eternity to know and appreciate all that has gone on before us and for us. The more we think and know about it, the more we should lift up our hands and heart in praise and continually shout, "Glory! Glory! Glory!"

Chapter 22

The Incredible Reward of Our Future Perseverance

We conclude our journey through the scriptures and hopefully retain the wonderful truth that God is for us as we are becoming more and more aware that we moving very fast to the end of time. The final curtain is soon going to close, and we need to consider what priorities we need to consider important. As I have been moving through my later years, I have not only reflected of the past, but I also find myself considering what my later years hold for me. One of the rewarding things about reflecting on my past sixty-seven years—which included being an evangelist and a number of years in the pastoral ministry, with twenty-two of those as a bible professor in a Christian liberal arts college - is seeing the goodness of God and his active, guiding hand throughout my life. Though there were wonderful rewards, there were also disappointments that made me consider quitting, giving up. However, I was always able to gain hope and persevere. I found this attitude of not giving up always opened a new hope to go on. I found that God was with me and for me.

Throughout this book, I have explored the importance of observing how God's perseverance continued to reach forward in His purpose of establishing His eternal plan for His people.

1. Trust in God's providence for our future as believers.

2. Continue to believe that God has big plans for your life and future.
3. Don't let your perspective of the world determine your future. God knows the beginning and the end, and at the right time He will raise you up to your future.
4. Realize that the Lord is always working around us, and He desires to work through us. People, places, provisions, and experiences are all under His guidance and care.
5. Dr. Henry T. Blackaby, in his book *Experiencing God*, implores readers to find out where God is at work and then to join him.
6. There are over one hundred verses about perseverance in the Bible. Consider some of the following verses that I have chosen as examples.

Being confident of this very thing, that He who has begun a good work in you will complete it until the day of Jesus Christ. (Phil. 1:6)

Brethren, I do not count myself to have apprehended; but one thing I do, forgetting those things which are behind and reaching forward to those things which are ahead, I press toward the goal for the prize of the upward call of God in Christ Jesus. (Phil. 3:13–14)

Let us hold fast the confession of our hope without wavering, for He who promised is faithful. And let us consider one another in order to stir up love and good works. Not forsaking the assembling of ourselves together, as the manner of some, but exhorting one another, and so much the more as you see the Day approaching. (Heb. 10:23–25)

Just remember that there is more power in the future to shape us than all the power in the past that has shaped us!

The Greatest Promise Ever Made to Us: Heaven

> And God will wipe away every tear from our eyes, there shall be no more death, nor sorrow, nor crying. There shall be no more pain, for the former things have passed away. And He who sat on the throne said, "Behold, I make all things new." Write, for these words are true and faithful. (Rev. 21:4–5)

When we received Christ, our destiny for the future had already begun. He has already put eternity in our hearts (Ecc. 3:11). We need to understand that God's eternal purpose is to restore the glory of His creation, which includes us. Our earthly lives are preparation for our heavenly lives. This again is evidence of what we have been constantly emphasizing: *God is for us!*

I am reminded of an illustration I discovered years ago that I want to share with you. A little old lady had a habit of going daily to God's throne room. As she approached the throne, she noticed three men standing together in a huddle. She politely said, "Good morning, gentlemen!" but they gave no response. She continued on to the throne, saying, "Good morning, Father!" to which He replied, "Good morning, daughter," and proceeded to fill her basket with good things. Later that afternoon, she repeated her visit, and again she noticed those same three men standing in their huddle. She again gave her greeting, "Good afternoon, gentlemen," but still she got no response. She proceeded to the throne. "Good afternoon, Father," she said, to which He again acknowledged her with "Good afternoon, daughter," and again He filled her basket. She repeated her trip in the evening, and as she neared the throne, she saw these same men in their huddle. She again greeted them, saying, "Good evening, gentlemen," repeating it several times, but there was no response. As she approached the throne, she inquired, "Father, before you fill my basket, I noticed throughout the day three men standing outside. Who are they?" The Father responded, "Daughter, don't be concerned. Those are three theologians trying to figure out how to approach Me!" (Origin unknown)

Heaven, the afterlife, and the world beyond will always be the milestones and rewards of our faith and Christ's fulfillment of His love and sacrifice for us. Just think of the final adventure and unfolding heaven beyond the galaxies and planets and suddenly experiencing the Godhead in all its glory. Think of the host of angels and the unfolding of all their ministry as described in Hebrews 1:14, expressing their ministry for God: "Are they not all ministering spirits sent forth to minister to those who will inherit salvation?" I wouldn't be surprised if, when we get to heaven, they might rehearse some of their times of ministering to our situations on earth. I'm sure we will stand in awe with our eyes and mouths wide open as we lift our voices in praise and adoration of God's work for and in us while on earth. God has been for us to the end. Whenever we feel downhearted and somewhat perplexed with our lives, we should take a moment to reflect on how God has and will be there for us in all situations. One of our greatest glories of heaven will be eternal freedom from sickness, pain, and disease. Think of all our time on earth that we live in fear of or suffering from pain, disease, and death. The apostle Paul spoke to this in Romans 8:21–22: "The creature itself also shall be delivered from the bondage of corruption into the glorious liberty of the children of God."

Conclusion

Imagine the joy of finally realizing the glorious promises of God regarding your future life in heaven. Perhaps you have realized through this study that the Bible is truly God's love story to us depicted throughout every recorded event. My goal was to expose you to the total message God was constantly revealing from the beginning to the end of all the various events; the ultimate action of God was intervening in each situation and bringing it into His purpose for His creation. What was and is the purpose of God?

> For God so loved the world that He gave His only begotten Son, that whoever believes in Him should not perish but have everlasting life. For God did not send His Son into the world to condemn the world, but the world through Him may be saved. (John 3:16–17)

I trust you have finally come to the conclusion after this study that God is for us, for you, for your loved ones, and for the whole world.

I am confident that the truth of God's Word being preached in our churches will still have an impact on our lives until Jesus Christ comes to receive God's people, whom He has redeemed for an eternal heaven. It will be a time of peace and joy. As we behold His face and see His welcoming, open arms, we will then fully understand how God wants to enfold us in His arms of eternal love.

I am certain there will be heavenly choruses ringing

throughout all of heaven followed by many praises for the joy of our salvation and the presence of our Savior, the Lord Jesus Christ. As we arrive in heaven, our fears and doubts will be turned to joy due to the fact that God has been for us and now we are together, forever.

The following song should encourage our faith as we continue to travel through this life toward our eternal abode with Christ.

> **We Will Not Be Shaken**
> Though the battle rages,
> we will stand and fight.
> Though the armies rise up against us on all sides,
> We will not be shaken,
> we will not be shaken,
> we will not be shaken,
> For we trust our God.

Because God is for us, we will discover that heaven is a wonderful place, full of glory and grace. We are going to see our Savior's face. Heaven is glorious; heaven is a wonderful place! I trust that as you have been reading this book, you have sensed the love of God that is constantly directed toward your eternal life, that you will pray and witness to your loved ones, and that they will realize as you have that God is for us and desires us to share His love and the glory that will be before us forever and forever.

The Joy of Having a Life of Peace in This World

I would like to conclude this book by encouraging you to believe that you can experience the very peace of God in this life knowing that God is for us.

> Therefore, having been justified by faith, we have
> peace with God through our Lord Jesus Christ.
> (Rom. 5:1)

> For He Himself is our peace, who has made both one, and has broken down the middle wall of separation. (Eph. 2:14)

> Jesus said, "Peace I leave with you; My peace I give you. I do not give you as the world gives. Do not let your hearts be troubled and do not be afraid." (John 14:27)

This gives us the assurance that God is not angry with us; He has made provision for our peace with Him. We are part of the family of God, and now all His dealings with us are for our good. He will never be against us because we have been inducted into His family. If there is one thing that we as individuals long for in this world today, it is peace. As we view the news every day, we hear of violence, war, terrorism, hurricanes, floods that have destroyed towns, and communities in which restoration is constantly needed. It is as if our world is suddenly moving toward an end and people everywhere are gripped with fear. Our future is in the hand of God, which has control of all things.

The final conclusion that God is for us now demands the obvious question for you to answer: *Am I responding in that my life is for and in God?*

My friend Josh McDowell, who is an internationally known speaker, author, and traveling representative of Cru (formerly Campus Crusade for Christ), became a close friend while we were in seminary. He, to this day, has a passion for people to hear about Jesus Christ but an even deeper concern that they make a commitment to Him and for Him. In light of this, he published an outstanding book entitled *Evidence that Demands a Verdict*. I would like to challenge you, in light of my purpose of this book, to pose the question with the understanding of the evidence that God is for us, *Am I ready to respond positively to this truth that I am committing to Him as my Savior and Lord?*

If you have not received Jesus Christ as your Savior and made

Him the center and purpose of your life, *do it now*. God is for us so that we can be for Him! Consider the words of this song written by Kurt Kaiser

> **Oh, How He Loves You and Me**
> Oh, how He loves you and me.
> He gave His life,
> what more could He give?
> Oh, how He loves you,
> Oh, how He loves me;
> Oh, how He loves you and me!
> Jesus to Calvary did go,
> His love for sinners to show.

When we received Christ, our destiny had already been decided. He has already put eternity in our hearts (Ecc. 3:11). We need to understand that God's eternal purpose is to restore the glory of His creation, which includes us. Our earthly lives are a preparation for our heavenly lives. This again is evidence that I have been constantly emphasizing—God is for us!

Bibliography

Adams, Jay. 1974. Pulpit speech. Philadelphia: Presbyterian and Reformed Publishing Company.

Alcorn, Randy. 2004. *Heaven.* Carol Stream, IL: Tyndale House Publishers Inc.

Blackaby, Henry T. 1990. *Experiencing God.* Life-way Press.

Bounds, E. M. *The Complete Works.*

Bryant, Dewayne. ApologeticPress.org. http://www.apologeticpress.org

Cairns, Earl E. 1954. *Christianity through the Centuries.* Grand Rapids, MI: Zondervan Publishing.

Chambers, Oswald. 1963. *My Utmost for His Highest.* Uhrichsville, OH. Barbour Publishing Inc.

"Chart of the English Bible." American Bible Society. New York.

Damen, Mark. 2016. "Early Christianity and the Church." History and Civilization course information.

DeYoung, Kevin. TheGospelCoalition.org. http://www.thegospelcoalition.org (prior to 2018)

Evans, Tony. 2009. *Book of Illustrations.* Chicago, IL. Moody Press.

Gonzalez, Justo L. 1984. *The Story of Christianity,* vol. 2. San Francisco, CA. Harper & Row Publishers.

Jeremiah, David. *Heroes of the Faith.*

Jeremiah, David. 2013. *The Jeremiah Study Bible.* Nashville, TN. Worthy Publishing.

Kittle, Rudolf and Paul E. Kahle (eds.). *The Holy Scriptures, According to the Masoretic Text Biblia Hebraica.* Referenced in Geisler, Norman L. and William E. Nix. 1979. *From God to Us.* Chicago: Moody Press.

LaSor, William Sanford and William B. Eerdmans. 1982. *Old Testament Survey*. Grand Rapids, MI

Latourette, Kenneth Scott. 1953. *A History of Christianity*. New York: Harper & Row Publishers.

"Oh, How He Loves You and Me." 1992. *Songs for Praise and Worship*. Word Music Inc.

US Department of Health and Human Services. May 1983. Abortion Surveillance Report.

Van Ness Myers, Philip. 1905. *Mediaeval and Modern History*. Boston: Ginn and Company.

Warwick, Dionne. Vocalist. "What the World Needs Now." Recorded in 1967.

"We Will Not Be Shaken." Hillsong Music Publishing

About the Author

Author George P. Kimber taps his knowledge and experience from nearly six decades as an evangelist, pastor, teacher, and professor to explain his study and observation throughout scripture of the marvelous fact that God is actively "for us." He points out that, in its entirety, the Bible from Genesis to Revelation demonstrates how God intervenes in history through various situations showing that He is for us because His eternal love is always directed toward humankind.

Eternal Love Means God Is for Us will encourage our journey as believers personally and our ministry as "the church" to evangelize with greater confidence, which is needed so much as the church is being challenged today as to its relevance. Jesus still commands the church: "All authority in heaven and on earth has been given to me. Therefore go and make disciples of all nations, baptizing them in the name of the Father and of the Son and of the Holy Spirit, and teaching them to obey everything I have commanded you. And surely I am with you always, to the very end of the age" (Matt. 28:19–20).

George P. Kimber has served as an evangelist and a pastor and has founded several churches. He earned two master's degrees and a doctoral degree from Ashland Theological Seminary in Ohio. He was formerly ordained as a minister with the International Church of the Foursquare Gospel and is currently an ordained minister with the Brethren in

Christ denomination, in which he taught for twenty-two years at Messiah College in Grantham, Pennsylvania. He also authored a book titled *Disciples of the Holy Spirit,* published by Westbow Press.

Printed in the United States
By Bookmasters